Dr. Krista Geller

The Power of Pets

How Animals Affect Family Relationships

VDM Verlag Dr. Müller

Impressum/Imprint (nur für Deutschland/ only for Germany)

Bibliografische Information der Deutschen Nationalbibliothek: Die Deutsche Nationalbibliothek verzeichnet diese Publikation in der Deutschen Nationalbibliografie; detaillierte bibliografische Daten sind im Internet über http://dnb.d-nb.de abrufbar.

Coverbild: www.purestockx.com

Verlag: VDM Verlag Dr. Müller Aktiengesellschaft & Co. KG
Dudweiler Landstr. 99, 66123 Saarbrücken, Deutschland
Telefon +49 681 9100-698, Telefax +49 681 9100-988, Email: info@vdm-verlag.de

Herstellung in Deutschland:
Schaltungsdienst Lange o.H.G., Berlin
Books on Demand GmbH, Norderstedt
Reha GmbH, Saarbrücken
Amazon Distribution GmbH, Leipzig
ISBN: 978-3-639-16015-4

Imprint (only for USA, GB)

Bibliographic information published by the Deutsche Nationalbibliothek: The Deutsche Nationalbibliothek lists this publication in the Deutsche Nationalbibliografie; detailed bibliographic data are available in the Internet at http://dnb.d-nb.de.

Cover image: www.purestockx.com

Publisher:
VDM Verlag Dr. Müller Aktiengesellschaft & Co. KG
Dudweiler Landstr. 99, 66123 Saarbrücken, Germany
Phone +49 681 9100-698, Fax +49 681 9100-988, Email: info@vdm-verlag.de

Printed in the U.S.A.
Printed in the U.K. by (see last page)
ISBN: 978-3-639-16015-4

The Power of Pets:

How Animals Affect Family Relationships

By

Krista Scott Geller

This study was designed to explore the importance a pet can have on someone's life, including ways a pet affects the relationships an individual has with other family members. This study assessed how pets can be influential in people's lives, especially with regard to the cultivation of family relationships and the development and maintenance of emotional stability. The opinions of pet owners were reviewed with regard to whether they felt their pets loved them and considered them a family member. Also evaluated was how a relationship with one's pet might have been similar to any other relationship within one's family, along with the extent that one's pet added harmony or discomfort to family relationships.

The following research questions guided this exploratory and qualitative study: (a) In what ways can a pet influence a person's life regarding family relationships? (b) In what ways can a pet replace or act as a beneficial substitute for other interpersonal and significant relationships? Specific attention was paid to how pets affect individuals in their family and various relationships between the family members, including the different roles the pet plays within family circumstances.

An open-ended, 12-question survey was distributed to six undergraduate classes, two at Radford University and four at Virginia Polytechnic Institute and State University. Individuals identified different pets in their lives, and in some cases, described several positive attributes about their pets in the context of a

personal anecdote about their pets and certain family relationships.

The results of this study showed that pets are an important aspect to many

families, and in several cases represent another "family member," or another "sister

or brother." Pets often serve as a relief of distress for families by listening to verbal

behavior, providing a best friend, encouraging family bonding, and acting as a

protector.

Table of Contents

The Power of Pets:

How Animals Affect Family Relationships

Chapter One: Introduction

Whether intended, planned, expected, or even hoped, pets can leave their paw prints on many special relationships. They can be seen as a best friend, an important other, or even a family member. Over 50% of households in the world have a pet (Beck, 1999; Fogle, 1983), yet there is little information in the research literature regarding the impact of pets on people and their family relationships. Greater attention and future research needs to be paid to the interaction of family members and their pets (Roberts, 1994).

Relationships between normal, non-institutionalized adults and their pets obviously exist, but there is little conclusive literature on the nature of such relationships. However, some relevant studies have been conducted (Davis & Juhasz, 1985). For example, it has been demonstrated that talking to and stroking one's pet is less arousing to the person's cardiovascular system then communicating with other people (Friedmann & Thomas, 1985). Plus, talking to a pet can be a therapeutic exercise (Brickel, 1985; Davis & Juhasz, 1985; Eckstein, 2000). Katcher (1981) reported that nearly all pet owners talk to their pets and almost half of these individuals confide in their pets. They tell their pets secrets. Children report having intimate talks with their pets on a routine basis (Davis & Juhasz, 1985).

Katcher and Beck (1996) found that more than 70% of adolescents reported they confide in their pets. Some people experience a decrease in blood pressure when talking to their pets, indicating a more relaxed state with pets than with people (Barone, 1998; Beck, 1999; Eckstein, 2000; Friedmann & Thomas, 1985; Serpell, 1996). As Spicer (1990) concludes, "Who else listens so well to irrational ranting and raving without once interrupting?" (p. 13).

A pet can be there when no one else seems to be; a pet can appear to listen when the rest of the world seems disinterested; a pet can offer unconditional love when love from people appears to be conditional. In many situations, communicating with a pet is very different than with a person. There are no disagreements, arguing, or interruptions. In fact, the pet often just sits there and seemingly hears everything (Beck, 1999). A pet can also be a special friend, providing an escape from the world, a diversion from disagreeable realities, and a means for avoiding disruptive negative thoughts (Beck, 1999; Brickel, 1985). This study explored the influence of pets in family relationships.

Purpose Statement

The purpose of this study was to explore the importance a pet can have on someone's life, including ways a pet influences the relationships its caretaker has with other family members. How and in what ways can a pet help a human develop or sustain emotional stability and ease loneliness? If so, what aspects of pet-human relationships make this possible?

Pets can decrease the loneliness and depression of owners by providing a source of companionship and affection (Entin, 1986; Friedmann & Thomas, 1985). In several questionnaire surveys of pet owners, researchers observed a common theme. Over 50% of pet owners reported they talk to their pets frequently, as if they

6

were people, and considered their pets to be sensitive to their moods (Friedmann & Thomas, 1985). This kind of attachment shows that when in need of close, affectionate contact with others, the family pet can be beneficial (Serpell, 1996). These kinds of close relationships with pets can help people cope with physical and psychological stressors in their everyday lives (Brickel, 1985; Serpell, 1996).

A pet can actually open communication lines between family members, especially when some family members rarely speak to each other except through their pets (Spicer, 1990). Some people relate better to pets than humans. But, the relationships with a human and a pet are often not as simple as might be expected. Human-pet relationships can be quite complex and help individuals deal with family crises and emotional distress (Entin, 1986). For example, Cain (1985) described a number of specific instances where a pet was instrumental in stabilizing a family. When family members experienced conflict, for example, a pet would do something "cute" which distracted family members from their disagreements. Moreover, pets can facilitate pleasure, fun, and exercise. Some pets are also used for security and protection, as well as a way to teach children responsibility and a respect for life.

Some respondents admitted they talk to their pets in lieu of other family members. In some cases they talked with a pet about a family member with whom they had interpersonal conflict, loud enough so the other family members could hear what they were saying. This form of communication reflects triangulation between the family members and the pet. It can open the lines of communication within a family. This may not be the best choice of communication, but in some cases it is all there is. Without the presence of a pet, communication might be even more limited (Spicer, 1990).

Research Questions

Pet and human interaction can be a positive, healthy and significantly dynamic in the lives of family members (Sussman, 1985). The pet can facilitate improvement in self-worth, interpersonal competence, life satisfaction, happiness, and marital health. Along with promoting positive interactions between family members, pets can add a substantial dose of genuine affection to the family (Spicer, 1990; Sussman, 1985). Pets can also serve as a social lubricant, increasing the quantity and improving the quality of interpersonal conversation. Pet-human interactions can supplement human-human interactions or even substitute for certain human relationships (Veevers, 1985).

The following research questions guided this exploratory and qualitative study:

(1) In what ways can a pet influence a person's life regarding family relationships?

(2) In what ways can a pet replace or act as a beneficial substitute for other interpersonal and significant relationships?

Specific attention was paid to how pets affect individuals in their family and various relationships between the family members, including the different roles the pet plays within family circumstances. The special significance of a pet as an actual "family member" was explored, including the degree to which human-pet relationships reduce feelings of anxiety, distress, and personal inadequacy (Bruner,

1983). Pets have been shown to promote self-assurance and adequacy, conveying positive regard for the owner and providing a special comfort that does not impose standards on a person's performance (Davis & Juhasz, 1985).

A variety of animals, including, birds, chinchillas, guinea pigs, hamsters, horses, ferrets, bunnies, snakes, cats, and dogs, serve as pets. In fact, most of the research literature in this area does not specify the kind of animal referred to as a "pet." The term used throughout the research reviewed is simply "pet," leaving the role of "pet" open to any possible animal. Dogs and cats are the most common animals playing the pet role in American culture. However, in this research pets were not defined as a dog or a cat. Participants were asked to list the pets they grew up with as an adolescent and to name the one pet that was most influential in their lives.

The Potential Downside of Pets

Even though pets have been discussed throughout this chapter as a positive influence in family life, they can also be an un-welcomed burden. Some studies have shown pets to have little beneficial impact on its owner's life. Some pet roles can be central to one person's life and well-being, but extraneous and insignificant to someone else's life (Davis & Juhasz, 1985). In some circumstances, pets can be barriers to constructive social interaction.

Some pets are actually used to keep others away. In one case, a man kept several snakes in his house in order to keep his relatives from visiting. Then there is the not unusual example of an elderly lady who surrounded herself with cats and dogs in order to maintain the excuse of being "too busy" to attend to other matters in her life or the lives of others. In some cases, pets can contribute to an unsanitary and unappealing residence, thereby preventing visits from other people. (Veevers, 1985).

Pets can also limit constructive communication between family members. This happens when a family member only speaks through a pet. Some people have explained that they would talk to a pet instead of a family member, thereby limiting interpersonal communication in the family (Spicer, 1990; Soares, 1985). In addition, pets can be the source of interpersonal conflict in a family (Soares, 1985). For example, how should a pet be disciplined? Who is the primary caretaker? Who cleans up after a pet? How much and what space can the pet have?

A pet can also promote negative relationships within the family. Consider how one couple's relationship ended because of a pet dog. The pair slept together every night with the dog between them, thereby limiting sexual contact and distancing the couple. When the dog passed away, the couple separated shortly afterwards. Apparently, this dog provided an excuse for their distance and emptiness. When the dog died, they lost the focus of their prior relationship and could not develop another (Entin, 1986).

There are also instances of violence against a family pet. Sometimes an aggressive impulse is taken out on the family pet instead of a family member. There is evidence that such behavior may be a precursor of subsequent violence towards other people. While aggression towards companion animals could serve as a substitute for aggression towards people, it can also be a kind of "practice" which can later escalate to more serious violence with others (Veevers, 1985).

The current research attempted to identify factors which contribute to positive versus negative influence of a pet in family relationships. Whether positive or negative, pets seem to significantly impact the lives of many, which in my case, proved to be one of the most positive experiences in my life as an adolescent.

A Personal Case Study

Animals have always been a significant part of my life. Ever since I was able to walk I was on the back of a pony and ever since I was able to beg I was asking for a kitten to hold. Pets have been a huge inspiration in my life, from socially opening me up to the world and offering a lasting friendship, to teaching me to cherish another life. I never realized what a positive affect pets had over me until I reflected on my most influential childhood pet--Goldie.

Writing about Goldie and the friendship we had when I was so young was helpful in understanding how much my life was positively influenced by a pet. This made me wonder how many other children had a special pet in their lives that brought them a friendship others could not. Discussing Goldie enabled me to understand the influence an animal can have on a child and how important a pet's unconditional affection can be.

Bringing all this together in a personal narrative motivated me to study systematically the potential impact of pets in other families. Reflecting on what Goldie added to my life suggests the special value a pet can have in other's lives. This personal narrative also allows me to evaluate the uncommon relationship I had with my cat and to explore how that relationship affected other relationships within

11

my family, including, the facilitation of my verbal interaction with others (Gergen, 1999).

It was actually one of those times when I put my hands on a stray cat and refused to let go, obligating my mother to bring him home. This was my pet cat-- Goldie. We did more then just play together, we grew up together. We shared a unique connection, a friendship so wonderful to me as a little girl that it seemed to contain the meaning of life. At least it made my life meaningful. Goldie wasn't just my cat, he was my most cherished companion whose presence seemed to fill every corner of my world with love and devotion. From my five-year-old perspective, he made a little girl smile when the rest of the world got her down.

It is not unusual for pets like Goldie to play a distinct role in the family (Cain, 1985). Goldie was there when I needed support, he was there to help me escape from a troubled day, and he was there when I felt all alone. He was a beloved pet that had all the comforting qualities of a best friend. He was my cat-- my special pet and my best childhood friend.

Goldie seemed to open up my world and other relationships in my life. He gave me the opportunity to express myself and my feelings to my family members and other people. I was able to convey my emotions to Goldie. He allowed me to express how I was really feeling, something I found hard to do with people. I was troubled when it came to communicating with others outside and within my family. I was never sure if what I was saying was how I really felt, and I was concerned that if I didn't really feel what I expressed, than others would never understand me.

I had a hard time communicating my emotions, but talking to my cat enabled me to:

a) understand my own feelings,

b) open up a discussion about how I really felt, and

c) practice verbalizing thoughts and ideas for later expression to family members.

Talking with Goldie gave me the confidence and self-efficacy to communicate within my family, disclosing my emotions and allowing my family members to learn about my feelings. Goldie brought me out of my shell. He provided me opportunities to express myself and develop communication skills for interaction with family members.

All this was taken away from me one very miserable morning. I remember it as if it had happened yesterday. It started with an incredible pain I felt inside which seemed to have progressed from the previous day. It was a pain that seemed to have no cause or purpose -- no reason to exist.

It began as a sick ache in my heart that just seemed to sit there, as if having hidden rationale, waiting to be exposed. That night I had gone to bed eagerly without saying goodnight to anyone, not even Goldie, as I had usually done every other night. The next morning I was expecting to feel relieved and rested, but instead I felt even more depleted and incredibly upset. It was as if I knew my entire adolescent life was about to change in some profound way.

When my mom pulled the car out of the driveway that morning, I saw the source of my unexplained heartache. I spotted a dull, wet orange-colored image on the lawn. I knew deep down what was over there, but finding the strength to look closer seemed impossible. My mother investigated and confirmed that the orange lifeless body was indeed Goldie's. All I could do at that point was go to school. In my mind that's what I had to do. That was the only way I would be able to wake up from the hideous nightmare I was experiencing. But school didn't help, instead things only got worse.

When I got to school I just sat expressionless in my first period class. This only attracted unwanted attention. When class started I didn't move. I remained with my backpack on my desk and the side of my face pressed into it. I had only one thought, "when will I wake up?" When one of my friends asked me if I was okay, I was hit with the reality that this nightmare was not a dream and would never end--I was living my nightmare.

My best little friend whom I cherished with all my heart, all my life, and the one I grew up with, was dead. He was never going to come back. Who was I going to talk to now? Who was going to make me feel better after a bad day at school, especially this one? All I could do was fall to the floor in hopes that I would hit hard enough to make the pain disappear. But it didn't. Instead the reality of my profound loss only became more absolute.

When the school day had finally ended and it was time to go home, I had to deal with the certainty that the little furry creature who was always there to greet me at the door and restart my day with a pleasant energy, wouldn't be there this time-- and every time to follow. Goldie, who was once filled with great vigor and love, was now a lifeless body tucked in a box. All I could was hold him closely and curse the world for taking my one and only (it seemed) true friend.

How was I going to get over this loss, this painful heartache? Was there any way I would be able to live without the one adoring friend who seemed to make everything so much better? He was my buffer to life's negative realities. He was the best communication tool I had within my family. He enabled me to reveal my deepest feelings, express me thoughts, and adjust my outlook on life. He provided therapeutic support for my seemingly overwhelming adolescent problems. To a young girl, this pet --a cat-- made every problem in the world seem understandable and solvable.

The day Goldie died was the day I learned more about myself than I could have ever imagined. I learned that I had developed the ability to communicate within my family, I learned that talking about my emotions is allowed and that others will listen, I also learned that I had a deep ability to love, and to feel loved, even by a simple cat. A pet that was not just important to me, but a cat that seemed to impact every individual in my family. What a rude awakening I experienced when Goldie left us. It seemed as though I lost critical support that I assumed would always be there-- a comfort zone I had always relied on.

I lived in a rural community without many other children, so finding a close friendship was difficult, if not impossible. It is not unusual for a pet owner to turn to a companion animal for intimate friendship and feelings of comfort and security when the preadolescent's social system cannot or does not meet the developmental needs of middle childhood (Davis & Juhaszz, 1985). Goldie acted as a substitute for other interpersonal relationships missing in my early life. He was my "peer support." With him I was able to talk out my problems, my emotions, and my daily thoughts.

By locating myself in the research process, I have used a case study to illustrate the potential power a pet can have on family relationships, to demonstrate how a pet can be positively intertwined within family life and drastically change a child's outlook. This personal story illustrates the value of human-pet communication which can spread to the family. It demonstrates how relationships within family and peers can be improved by a caring friendship with a pet.

This story explicates the purpose for the current research, not just because the relationship I had with a pet affected my life so profoundly, but because so many other lives have probably been similarly influenced. Finding commonalities between such human-pet relationships could enable increased understanding of the roles a pet can have in families and reveal distinct therapeutic value in developing such relationships.

Chapter Two

Theoretical Framework and Literature Review

Theoretical Framework

This chapter presents a review of the literature related to human-pet relationships in a family, including a discussion of the theory of symbolic interaction as it relates to human-pet communication.

Symbolic Interactionism

Symbolic interaction, the theory guiding this study, is a useful theoretical perspective for understanding the family and other social worlds (Klein & White, 1996; LaRossa & Reitzes, 1993). Humans are motivated to create "meanings" to help them make sense of their world. These meanings might be given to them by a pet who motivates them to engage in a relationship that is beneficial to the individual and the family (Klein & White, 1996; Netting et al., 1987).

There are certain symbols and words humans express to one another that are recognized as meaningful. Symbolic interaction is essentially "a frame of reference for understanding how humans, in concert with one another, create symbolic worlds and how these worlds, in turn, shape human behavior" (LaRossa & Reitzes, 1993, p. 136). Symbolic interactionism represents "a diverse family of theories, and it can be difficult to detect what many of these variants now have in common that unites them under a single banner" (Klein & White, 1996, p. 89).

People communicate with symbols which are signs that are agreed upon and known to others. For example, the universal symbol "dad" stands as a sign for a particular person in our lives. Symbolic interactionism focuses on how these

17

symbols are shared (Klein & White, 1996). People have different symbols to represent their pets. For example, the name of a pet can be a very important symbol. Whether the pet understands its name or not, the name is often the most significant representation for the pet because in many cases, the name of the pet influences the nature of its relationship with humans. A dog named "Killer," for example, typically conveys expectation of unfriendly contact, whether or not such a label is warranted. Thus, the name of a pet can be a sign of communication, and along with the tone of voice from the owner, can suggest happiness, anger, or indifference towards the pet.

Two assumptions of symbolic interactionism relate directly to this study. One relates to the fact that humans act toward things according to the meaning those things have for them (LaRossa & Reitzes, 1993). A pet can fulfill a meaning of importance to an individual, even becoming as important as a spouse, "and in some instances act as surrogate mates" (Beck & Katcher, as cited in Veevers, 1985, p. 21).

The second assumption of symbolic interactionism identifies the process of interaction between people, communicating and being involved in a social situation (LaRossa & Reitzes, 1993). In some cases, the pet may serve as a conversational link that helps people interact with each other, thereby facilitating socialization (Netting et al., 1987). The drama of a social interaction can result from individuals feeling others are assessing their self-presentation (LaRossa & Reitzes, 1993). Sometimes talking to a pet is preferred because of the embarrassing or stressful situations that can result from human-human interactions. Individuals can feel

18

pressure to live up to an identity other people expect to see in them (LaRossa & Reitzes, 1993), but communicating with a pet does not include such complications. Socializing with the family pet can be uncomplicated, straightforward, and honest--with no strings attached (Netting et al., 1987; Sable, 1995).

Being able to talk with the family pet might be preferred because of misunderstandings or controversy that results from communicating with a family member. Misinterpretations in human relationships can be vast because perceptions are so personal and readily biased, leading to confusion, misunderstanding, and conflict. Thus, communicating with another human being can seem to be more of a burden than a benefit. In fact, we often avoid talking to someone because of anticipated distress or conflict. However, communication is central to family life, and being able to express one's feelings with family members is critical for healthy relationships (Fitzpatrick & Ritchie, 1993).

Communication defines family roles, which in turn determine peoples' ability and motivation to fulfill those roles. Of course, individuals add their own uniqueness to family roles. If a person ends up with multiple roles, then that person conveys and receives multiple expectations. A social role is defined by the accepted expectations for that status or position. A person's ability to communicate effectively often influences that individual's particular role in a social situation (Klein & White, 1996). Since pets don't have expectations about a person's social role, interaction with a pet can be less threatening than some interactions with humans (Davis & Juhasz, 1985).

Owners turn to their pets for regular companionship, which can become an interdependent and indispensable friendship (Davis & Juhasz, 1985). This research assessed how owners communicate with their pet and how that pet communicates back to them. There are several ways a pet can affect the communication within a family (Spicer, 1990). This research explored ways in which interacting with a pet reflects a significant relationship in the owner's life. How does a pet affect relationships with family members? Does a pet facilitate or hinder interaction with family members? Does a pet bring family members together or drive them apart?

Communication Roles

Communication is a key to any healthy relationship, and in some cases a pet facilitates communication. The pet can often open the lines of conversation for a family in various ways. They can provide an active or passive medium for interpersonal verbalization, or give people something to talk about (Davis & Juhasz, 1985; Friedmann & Thomas, 1985; Spicer, 1990). Pets can also take on certain roles within a family that in turn affect interpersonal communication. For instance, pets can provide the kind of friendship that offers companionship and affection for an individual (Entin, 1986; Friedmann & Thomas, 1985). Pets can assume the role of best friend, the surrogate mate, the caretaker, the listener. Indeed, a pet can play many different roles, each accompanied by profound feelings (Sussman, 1985).

In our society, each stage of a person's life can be characterized by several varying and changing roles (Netting, Wilson, & New, 1987). A role can be viewed as any set of behaviors that has some common accepted definition (Netting et al., 1987). Four dimensions characterize the social impact of roles: 1) the number of roles per individual, 2) the intensity of the role involvement, 3) the pattern of participation in a role, and 4) the degree of structure imposed by the role (Netting et al., 1987).

Children have fewer and very differing roles than adults. Some authors claim every child should own a pet, and take on the various roles required to care for an animal (Netting et al., 1987). Young children can develop a sense of responsibility when caring for a pet, and the preadolescent owner might identify his or her pet as "something that makes me feel good about myself" (Davis & Juhasz, 1985, p. 91). In some situations the pet can be a replacement for some other significant relationship. Some children have limited playmates when growing up, and the pet serves as the ideal playmate for those children (Netting et al., 1987).

Understanding Pets in the Family

Human-family interaction is often facilitated by the family pet. In fact, the role of the family pet is often determined by the structure of the family, which can include the emotional strengths and weaknesses of each family member, the social climate of the family, and emotional undercurrents within the family (Soares, 1985). Actually, the family photo album can provide resourceful insight to help families understand their relationships with each other and with their pets. Frequency and location of a pet in the family pictures is often a good indicator of the relative importance of the pet to the family as a whole, as well as significance of the pet per each person in the family (Entin, 1986).

Pets allow for human-human interaction in several different ways. The most common ways are within the social circle. A pet can stimulate communication and social contact between people because of the approachability a pet provides another person. Just seeing another person with a pet can often facilitate a conversation. After asking a few questions about the pet, the interaction can readily transition to longer social discussions (Beck, 1999).

Pets can satisfy the need to feel important. They can function as an ego-extension for an individual related to self-esteem (Davis & Juhasz, 1985; Brickel, 1985). A pet can also positively affect an individual's self-esteem or self-image by being a loyal friend or by eliminating loneliness (Davis & Juhasz, 1985; Beck, 1999).

Pets can often take on therapeutic stances that allow an individual to work out conflicts within themselves and present an opportunity for individuals to try on new roles within their family (Brickel, 1985). They encourage touch and care and also permit people to laugh at themselves and their surroundings, which in some cases can reduce the stressors in a particular situation (Beck, 1999).

As a playmate for children, a pet contributes substantially to an individual's healthy progression into adulthood. Caring for a pet cultivates personal responsibility while also building a useful animal-human bond (Brickel, 1985; Davis & Juhasz, 1985). The family is a primary agent for exposing children to animals and instilling in them respect and love for animals. Families teach children to relate emotionally to animals. Often the pet reciprocates by teaching the child about constructive interaction while providing a rewarding, uniformly positive experience (Brickel, 1985).

Review of the Relevant Literature

My review of the recent literature on family relationships uncovered minimal objective information on the value of pets in normal family functioning. Numerous articles address the varied roles of pets with the physically challenged, but few studies have addressed relationships between able-bodied people, especially with regard to the impact of pets on family interactions.

Articles in three sources, *The Family Journal, Social Work Journal, Anthrozoos Journal,* and one book chapter in *Pets and the Family* addressed the pet as a positive facilitator for family relationships and a teacher of responsibility for children. In all four studies, researchers discussed the results of surveys which had been given to pet owners, asking their opinions of pets and how important the pet is to their family. These studies addressed the pets' attachment and well-being across the life cycle of the human-pet bonding experience. Each article had its own unique explanation for the importance of pets, but each concluded that pets are usually a healthy addition to any family. Although there is vast research literature on the family as an interaction system dependent on interpersonal communication, most of this literature excludes the pet as part of the family system. Thus, the impact a pet can have on family members and their relationships has only been infrequently examined systematically.

As concluded by Soares (1985) "there are, in fact, only a few studies of normal human/companion animal interaction, and even fewer that examine this relationship in the context of the family" (p. 50). In addition, "the psychosocial relationship between the young and pets is not a widely researched topic"

(MacDonald, as reported in Davis & Juhasz, 1985, p. 79). In contrast, studies that deal with how a pet can influence the lives of the elderly are much more common.

It is typical for pets to be considered a family member (Brickel, 1985; Davis & Juhasz, 1985; Soares, 1985). For example, Cain (1983) found that 87% of her sample of 896 families considered their pet a member of their family, and 36% thought of their pet as another person. In addition, Voith (1983) surveyed 500 dog owners and found 99% to consider their dog a family member.

Emotional Support

Pets can show a unique concern for a human that only the owner truly understands. Emotional empathy "is the vicarious emotional response to another's emotions or states, and is regarded as distinct from perspective taking, which involves the cognitive comprehension of another's thoughts and feelings" (Paul, 2000, p. 194). Emotional empathy has been considered to apply equivalently to human and animal targets because it has been regarded as so broadly applicable (Paul, 2000).

Most people who are empathetic and caring in their views of animals will likely have the same sentiments toward people. Past and present ownership of a pet can lead to greater concern about the treatment and welfare of animals (Paul, 2000). Paul (2000) showed that those respondents who had owned pets during their childhood had significantly higher animal-oriented empathy scores than those who did not have a pet during childhood.

Brickel (1985) examined how individuals acquire and maintain an emotional bond for animals throughout their lifetime. He found that some people perceive

24

animals as emotional wards in the family. Both Brickel and Larsen et al. (1974) suggest that, "empathy for pets may be greater than for other people" (p. 42). It seems intuitive that bonding with a pet can often be easier and less complicated than with another person.

Eckstein (2000) developed "The Pet Relationship Impact Inventory," and found two different types of people, "those who love and adore pets as regular members of the family, and those who do not" (p. 192). The pet self-assessment questionnaire was offered to families who completed it as a group. Interestingly, the size of the family, the structure of the family, the mother's employment status, and the children's attitude toward pets influenced whether the family had a household pet. It was also discovered that "the emotional bond and desire for proximity between children and pets is congruent with attachment behavior towards humans, yet the relationship between child and pet is considered simpler and less conflicted than human relationships" (p. 196).

Additionally, pets have been described as serving the function "of a living security blanket for children" (Eckstein, 2000, p. 196). For many children, the pet is responsible for providing an emotional attachment that can be created through the deep bond of affection that comes from loving and being loved by a pet (Eckstein, 2000). Pets can become an essential aspect of early bonding and attachment for children. They not only provide a median for a child's verbal and nonverbal communication exchange, they also provide security, emotional support, and most importantly—unconditional love (Eckstein, 2000).

Entin (1986) discussed unique insights into the emotional process of the family offered by animal companionship. Pets function "as part of the emotional process of the family" (Entin, 1986, p. 13). Davis and Juhasz (1985) showed in their survey research how some young adults can find it easier to communicate with a pet and express their emotions with a pet rather a person, because the young person "feels safe in communicating to a pet and trusts the animal" (p. 83).

A Powerful Role

Cain (1985) describes the valuable role a pet plays in the family system. "Pets serve as positive purposes in the family such as a means for pleasure, fun, and exercise, as a source of physical security and protection, as a means of teaching children responsibility and a respect for life" (p. 5). The results of a 32-item questionnaire based on pets and the family, completed by 896 families, indicated that families considered their pets to be very important to them. In fact, 93% of the respondents had pets while growing up, 99% reported they thought children should have pets, 98% considered their pet a family member or a close friend. Moreover, 72% said their pet usually had "people status" in the family.

Pets change the nature of family interactions. Of the total pet owners, 70% reported an increase in family happiness and fun after getting a pet, 60% indicated an increased expression of affection around the pet, and 52% said family together time increased with a pet. When asked what special characteristics their pet displayed, 77% of the 896 respondents believed their pet understood when they talked or confided in them. One person even claimed her pet was a "live-in-psychiatrist" (p. 7). Moreover, 73% reported their pet communicated back to them, and 59% believed their pet understood them and was sensitive to their moods (Cain, 1985).

Also reported by Cain (1985) were examples on how a pet can break tension in a household. He described situations when the pet acted as a peacemaker, and in one case a dog was described as a diversion from a crisis. There were also times when the pet would do something "cute" and people would forget they were angry, or occasions when the pet requested attention during periods of tension. There were even situations in which the pet seemed to sense anger and did something silly to make people laugh. This kind of "pet-therapy" helped family members develop a sense of balance again. Paying attention to the pet allowed them to reflect on their perceptions and get control of their feelings (Cain, 1985).

Humanizing Pets

Veevers (1985) reported that "if dependent populations benefit from animal companions, might not healthy adults do so as well?" (p. 12). Veevers (1985) discusses the social roles companion animals can play in contemporary society and the influence of those roles.

Pets have become humanized. Most grooming services offered for a human can now be received by a pet. For example, poodles regularly get their hair done at beauty parlors, which includes a shampoo, a cut, a blow-dry, and a manicure. Sometimes when poodles arrive at these parlors they travel by limousine while wearing a custom-made sweater. Expensive and attractive pets are often viewed as a personal accessory, just like an expensive car or diamond ring (Veevers, 1985).

Because of the strong amount of affection expressed by a pet, a pet can be a replacement or a surrogate for a human relationship. Some childless couples consider their pets to be their children--loving their pets as they would their own children. A pet can also serve as a surrogate parent, enabling the child to practice a variety of interactions with the pet which can later be incorporated into other social relationships.

It is likely the role a pet plays in someone's life determines the nature of the influence the pet has for that person. Roles vary in their relations to social positions. There are different roles set within a family and these roles change periodically, depending upon the shared norms within the family (LaRossa & Reitzes, 1993). Pets often have their own identity within a family and can be an extension of a family member.

As with symbolic interactionism, pets can contribute substantially to human interdependency. From this perspective, "thinking, knowing, believing, and self-understanding, all have their origins in social interchange" (Gergen, 1999, p. 124). When communicating with a pet it's not necessary to hide your identity. In contrast, when exchanging feelings with a human it's often necessary to take the role of the other person in order to communicate effectively (Gergen, 1999, p. 124). This can cause distress. Connecting with a pet, on the other hand, has been considered simpler and less stressful (Eckstein, 2000).

Summary

This chapter reviewed the impact a pet can have on family members and the interactions within the family system. The minimal research on the impact of pets in a family suggests that pets are valuable to a family, providing attention, therapy, surrogate support, and instructive relationships. Pets are usually considered family members with an adoring and positive attachment that can bring great significance to the relationships within the family. However, these notions are speculative and the related research is exploratory at best.

The current study adds to the little research available on pet-human relationships in family situations. The focus will be on how pets influence a person's life by contributing to or detracting from relationships. Also addressed is whether the pet acts as a substitute for any other relationships and the positive vs. negative impact of such substitutions. As reviewed above, a pet can often serve many different roles in the family, thereby intensifying and complicating various family relationships (Netting, Wilson, & New, 1987). This study attempts to define such roles.

The more attached family members are to a pet, the more functional the family system is in terms of cohesion and adaptability. The family pet might also reflect the family emotional system, in the same way the family members' behaviors reflect emotional reactivity (Roberts, 1994). The changing landscape of family life in the 21st century will likely increase the importance of pets in the family and their ability to reduce loneliness, define a purpose to life, and provide the consistent contact comfort of a friend (Sable, 1995).

Chapter Three

Methodology

Overview of the Study

The present study explored the importance a pet can have on someone's life, particularly ways a pet impacts the relationships that person has with other family members. I wanted to know how pets can be influential in people's lives, especially with regard to the cultivation of family relationships and the development and maintenance of emotional stability. I assessed the opinions of pet owners regarding whether or not they felt their pets loved them and whether or not their pets were considered a family member. Also assessed was how a relationship with one's pet might have been similar to any other relationship within one's family. I assessed the extent that one's pet added harmony or discomfort to family relationships.

Data Collection Process

Pilot Study

A pilot study was conducted to develop and refine the survey. This process was necessary because no other published studies could be found on the same topic. The pilot survey, included in Appendix C, was distributed to a small class of 26 undergraduate students and collected after 15 minutes. The survey was then revised and improved according to the answers provided.

As detailed above, the revised survey, included in Appendix A, was distributed to six undergraduate classes with approximately 25 students in each class. The participants were informed that completing the survey is voluntary and deciding not to participate would be inconsequential.

The participants were 102 college students enrolled in six university classes, four at Virginia Tech and two at Radford University. They were asked to reflect upon the most influential pet in their lives and the various ways that pet was advantageous or disadvantageous to their family relationships. In anticipation of conducting this study, I have reflected on the most influential family pet in my life, and as a result, explored ways in which that pet facilitated my emotional and social development. The college students in the present study were asked to do the same.

The participants contemplated and expressed the influence a particular pet(s) had in their lives. Many college students have had the opportunity to own a few pets, and have experienced numerous family relationships in which a pet was influential. Although most of the respondents do not currently live at home, they were able to describe their home experiences and the critical family roles fulfilled by their pets.

As Bogdan and Biklen (1998) explain, the process of personal reflection is the self-revealing of a person's view of experiences. Such reflection provides detailed evidence, of the meaning participants assign to certain situations with a pet(s). This method of reflection also allows for a better understanding of how an individual and their family might be affected through their pet(s). Taking the time and assessing my own pet experiences has permitted me to open my mind up to the events others might have encompassed. This procedure encourages an exploration into the incidents of peoples' lives and the beliefs they hold true about their own pet(s). A rich quality to each question is then retained allowing me to discover such themes and concepts which explain the importance of a pet to that individual and their family, offering a meaning to each story and concept discovered (Bogdan & Biklen, 1998). Personal documents also allow an introduction to the emotional and social development facilitating an appreciation for the impact a pet might have provided for the participant and his/her family life. This allows for further examination of ones' own self, providing a meaning that might not have been understood or grasped before (Bogdan & Biklen, 1998).

I asked these college students to choose a pet (if any) that was most influential in their lives-- one that had an impact on their family relationships (see Appendix A for a copy of the survey). I also inquired about how that pet influenced their family interactions and determined, from their responses, if that pet was an inhibitor or a facilitator of various interactions within their family. I wanted the participant to recall a pet they felt was most influential in their lives, whether as an adolescent or as an adult. I encouraged the participants to acknowledge the influence this pet had on their family, including the time (i.e., their age) when this pet was most significant.

The participants were not representatives of any particular group, but were a convenience sample consisting of students from undergraduate classes at Radford University and Virginia Polytechnic Institute and State University. An open-ended survey was distributed to six different undergraduate classes: two classes were at Radford University and four classes were at Virginia Polytechnic Institute and State University. (See Appendix A for the open-ended survey, Appendix B for the pilot survey, and Appendix C for the responses, as transcribed verbatim for the 102 completed surveys).

The surveys were distributed to all the students in the class, allowing them the option to decline participating in the study. No incentive (e.g., extra credit toward a course grade) was offered, and a participant could voluntarily cease completing the survey at any time. Three of the undergraduate classes at Virginia Polytechnic Institute and State University had the option of taking the survey home with them and returning it the next class meeting.

Description of the Sample

Table 3.1 describes the sample of participants with regard to age and gender. Six age categories are represented with a majority of students being 21 (n=42) and 20 (n=28). The sample consisted of more females (n=78) than males (n=24).

Table 3.1

Ages of Sample by Gender

Age	19	20	21	22	23	24	Total
Male	0	7	8	8	1	0	24
Female	9	21	34	10	2	2	78
Total	9	28	42	18	3	2	102

Analysis of the Data

The primary analysis strategy was a qualitative content analysis--defined as "the study of particular aspects of the information contained in a document, film, or other form of communication" (Gall, Borg, & Gall, 1996, p. 756). Considered were relevant concepts from the theoretical framework of symbolic interaction, which guided the research. The particular research questions chosen and mentioned earlier shaped the data collection, along with my own personal thoughts and passion about pets that ignited and fueled this exploratory study.

In consultation with my advisor, I numbered the surveys and read each one seven times, looking systematically for common themes and placing the answers in discrete categories for meaningful comparisons (i.e., family bonding provided by pet, self-esteem booster, unconditional love, easing of stress, and the "best friend" attributed to many). Each response to every question was typed up and compiled, as included in Appendix D, which was checked over twice and edited to make sure everything that was written in the surveys was correctly transcribed.

To check for reliability, my advisor was also given a copy of the numbered survey's and Appendix D to read, to compare notes, and to check for themes and concepts. As the surveys were read, consistent themes and concepts emerged, revealing rather repetitious opinions of most respondents.

These themes represent the different kinds of impact a pet had on the participants' relationships within the family and as an individual. Patterns in how the participants responded were considered and evaluated. Some participants were not affected by their pet as strongly as others, but each participant had something positive to say about some pet they had in their lives. Six participants did not have pets, but three of these respondents were affected in a beneficial way by the presence of someone else's pet. In any case, individuals reacted uniquely to their pets-- some enjoyed the relationship a great deal, others were not as affected, as Netting et al., (1987) found in their study of the human-animal bond.

I asked the participant to write his or her age when their family pet was most influential in their lives. In many cases, the participants related back to their adolescence through their adulthood and discussed different influential pets throughout their childhood development. Several participants wrote that their family pet taught them the deep bond of attachment that comes from loving and being loved, validating evidence from my own personal narrative in Chapter 1. As Eckstein (2000) describes, the relationship between child and pet may be easier to establish and causing less conflict than human-human relationships.

Careful comparisons of all themes and patterns were made across each participant. I was able to examine the similarities and differences between each individual's experiences with their pet as a significant other (LaRossa & Reitzes, 1993), as well as how the pet added to the pleasures of their life and gave them a feeling of comfort and companionship when times were tough.

Chapter Four

Results

The results are based upon 102 open-ended, written surveys that were
distributed to six different undergraduate classes, two at Radford University and
four at Virginia Polytechnic Institute and State University. The survey was
designed to explore the influence of pets in family life, particularly, how they affect
a person's relationships with other family members. The survey was also designed
to assess the ways a pet can replace or act as a beneficial substitute for interpersonal,
significant relationships beyond one's immediate family.

As I explored the answers on the surveys from the participants, several
themes emerged. It was obvious that pets are an extremely important ingredient in
many families. In fact, most participants described their pet as an actual family
member. In this chapter, the themes that emerged from the 12 survey questions are
discussed. First, I will begin by present the findings on the participants who did not
have pets. These individuals provided opinions and reactions to not having a pet.

Participants without Pets

Of the 102 participants, only six participants (three females and three males)
never had a pet. Participant 3 had this to say about not having a pet when he was
growing up:

> I always wanted a pet growing up, but mom kept saying no. I think I am still
> a little upset by her refusal to even consider having one.

Another participant with no pet shared the following perspective:

> I think that having a pet in the family adds a sense of unity to a family since
> they share a common task. I think my family would have been more relaxed
> in general if we had had a pet.

Each of these quotes indicates perceived importance of a pet even without the direct experience. Furthermore, Participant 4 expressed how she received pet benefits through her friends and their pets, even though she never had a pet of her own:

> My best friend when I was 11 had a black lab named Sam. We played with Sam everyday. We were there when she had puppies and tried to convince my parents to adopt one. My ex boyfriend in high school had cats and we'd play with them.

Participant 4 also expressed resentment towards her parents for not letting her have a pet. Specifically, she explained that not having a pet,

> "only caused stress and resentment that we couldn't have one."

These quotations communicate how pets can even have impact on individuals who did not actually have the opportunity to own a pet while they were growing up. Whether there was resentment in the house towards the parents for not letting a pet in the family, or just being able to find friends that had a pet and spend time with them, it is apparent that even non-owners of a pet perceive advantages of having a pet.

Type of Pet

The remaining 96 participants answered Question 2, i.e., "If yes to Question 1, how many and what kind of pet(s) did you have?" They listed the type and quantity of pets they had while growing up. Table 4.1 depicts the different types of pets that were listed on the survey, along with the number of people who had owned that particular kind of pet. Of these 96 participants, 84 listed having more than one pet in their lifetime.

There were twenty-two different types of pets listed on the surveys. The most prominent pets were the dog (n=81) and the cat (n=62). Fish were also mentioned relatively often as an influential pet in the family (n=28). Of the 96 participants who said they had a pet, only 12 mentioned having one pet. In these cases the pet was either a dog or a cat. There were many unusual animals listed as pets, including a mouse, an anole, a few hermit crabs and even a squirrel. Please see the following table which lists the number of people who had various types of pets.

Table 4.1

Type of Pet and the Number of People who had that Particular Pet

Type of Pet	Number of People with Pet	Percentages of Sample
Dog	81	76.5%
Cat	62	60.8%
Fish	28	27.5%
Hamster	15	14.7%
Bird	13	12.7%
Bunny	11	11.4%
Guinea Pig	11	11.4%
Frog	6	6.3%
Hermit Crab	5	5.2%
Turtle	5	5.2%
Horse	3	3.1%
Iguana	3	3.1%

Table 4.1 (continued)

Type of Pet	Number of People with Pet	Percentages of Sample
Gerbil	2	2.1%
Pig	2	2.1%
Lizard	2	2.1%
Mice	2	2.1%
Anole	1	1%
Cow	1	1%
Donkey	1	1%
Duck	1	1%
Sheep	1	1%
Squirrel	1	1%

Pets in the Family

Question 4 asked, "How well were pets perceived and treated in your family?" Every one of the 96 respondents described their pet(s) as being treated very well, along with several descriptions of how that pet(s) was treated and appreciated by the family. Participant 7 stated his pet as being treated,

"like one of the family."

Participant 14 also described his pet was as a family member:

> Very well, treated as almost a member of the family. Scruffy has frequented a certain chair (a lazy boy) so often it has become "his chair."

Forty one participants (42.7%) described their pets as being treated like one

of the family, and actually considered them to be a family member. Eight

participants said their pet was seen as their younger brother or sister, or their

parents' other child. In many cases, the pet was treated better than the family

members.

Participant 43 said this about her dog "Bingo:"

> We treated Bingo as if she was a part of the family. She was definitely my
> best friend. She always slept with me. My family gave her unconditional
> love.

Pets were frequently described as being a good form of companionship

which allowed for family bonding. The pets even received special gifts on holidays.

For example, Participant 93 commented,

> "they were treated well and were like my parents' children."

Special attention was not just given to a dog or cat, but also to other unique

pets, even fish. Participant 43 describes her routine when feeding her fish:

> We loved them. Feeding them and caring for them was a family ordeal. We
> even said "grace" before we sprinkled the fish flakes into their bowl.

Many (n=36) described their pets being treated as part of the family as

exemplified by the following research from Participant 102,

> like kings ☺ they're treated just like one of the family! If I got eggs, they
> got eggs.

Influential Pets

Question 5 asked, "Was there a particular pet that was most influential in

your life? What kind of pet was it? How old were you?" Of the 96 participants

who reported owning a pet, only 14 (14.6%) reported their pet(s) did not play an influential role in their lives. The remaining 82 had several positive and encouraging stories to tell about their most influential pet. For example, Participant 36 reported this about her dog,

> Yes, I got a Jack Russell Terrier last February and he is the biggest joy of my
> life.

Even a fish was seen as an influential pet for Participant 43:

> Yes, my beta fish, I loved it because it looked like a rainbow. I got it when I was 8, and it died when I was 14.

The 82 participants (86%) who had influential pets in their lives named the pets, their age, and in some cases, added a positive evaluation statement, as exemplified by this comment from Participant 41:

> My dog Maggie. She's a Yorkshire terrier and I got her for my 16th birthday. I'm her mommy!

Participant 59 talked about her cat as being her most influential pet when she was young and still has her to this day:

> Yes- my cat Kelsey- she is now old---12! She was never liked by the other cats- I'm her only true friend- we're like sisters! We got her when I was 10.

Participant 60 explained the special relationship she had with her cat:

> Nora-a mackerel tabby (cat). I was ten years old when she died of feline leukemia-she was such a good cat. We put her to sleep in my arms.

Significant Relationships

Question 6 asked, "Did this pet act as a significant relationship in your life, if so, in what ways?" Thirteen pet owners responded "no" to this question, and nine did not answer it. The 74 remaining pet owners (77.1%) reported a significant role was played by their pets. For example, Participant 27 explained:

"She is like my sister."

Twenty respondents described their pet as being a best friend in their lives. For example, Participant 25 mentioned this about her "best friend:"

> Yeah, she was my protector and my best friend when at home because I didn't have siblings.

Participant 44 echoed:

> She was my dog and I raised her from the minute I got her. She was always protective of me and my best friend.

Nine participants described their pet as being comforting, especially when they were sad. Participant 54 shared:

> He would always lay on the bed with me, I could even use him as a pillow. He seemed to follow me when I was upset and would sit while I cried, he was a comfort to me through childhood.

Eight participants said their pet listened to them when they were upset and explained how their pet was there for them when they needed to talk. Participant 102 portrayed her pet by saying:

> "Yes, he was and still is my confidence, the one I turn to when I want to talk." Participant 56 also confirmed:

> Bingo was definitely my best friend. I would talk to her when I had a problem, and she always looked at me as if she understood.

Seven participants depicted their pet as always being there for them-- their buddy when in need. Consider, for example, this statement from Participant 31:

> He was a god-send because I had just broken up with my boyfriend of 2 years, and Rudy filled that void for me.

Similarly, Participant 55 said this about her pet:

> Yes, companionship, sweet, I spent a lot of time caring for her. She laid with my mom in bed for 4 years while she was sick.

Several quotations affected personal dependency on the pet. In other words, it was not that the pet needed them, but they needed their pet, often as a stabilizing factor in their lives. This was revealed in the following statement from Participant 82 who said her pet was:

> Just fun loving, never gave us problems and she would always run to me when I cried.

Pets within the Family

Question 7 asked, "How have pets affected you and the relationship you had within your family (i.e., help with communication between family members, cause or help with stress in the family)?" Of the 96 participants, only 10 answered "no" to this question and 4 did not answer it. The remaining 82 (85.4%) had a variety of things to say about how their pets influenced relationships within their families. Twenty three participants said their pet reduced stress in their family, as exemplified by this perspective from Participant 100:

> They are a definite stress release when things get tense, just petting them relaxes the situation.

Eleven participants said their pets facilitated communication between family members. For example, Participant 102 affirmed:

> To keep up with the responsibilities of taking care of them, we've had to all learn to communicate and work together.

Eight participants who described their pets as bringing their family closer together, as reflected in this statement from Participant 50:

> Think they help with communication, give you something to talk about, reduce stress and tension.

Similarly, Participant 61 mentioned that his pets helped with,

"Communication, and when the dogs passed, my parents helping me through it." This illustrates that even a tragedy with a pet can bring a family closer. Four participants described their pet as teaching them responsibility, as noted by Participant 95:

> They helped us as children learn responsibility, we had to communicate to our parents the responsibilities we would take on before we were allowed to get the pet.

Likewise, Participant 63 remarked that his pet:

> Has increased the bond because my parents love Chance just as much as me and have no problem caring for him if something comes up with me, nothing negative.

Negative Experiences

Question 8 asked, "Did you ever have a negative experience with a pet?" Of the 96 respondents, 33 (34.3%) reported never having a negative experience. Of the 61 participants who did convey a negative experience, 26 (42.6%) indicated their only negative experience occurred when their pet died. For example, Participant 8 said:

> "when they died, as they inevitably did, that was pretty negative."

Eleven respondents said their most negative experience was being bitten by a pet. Such as a negative experience in epitomized by the following from Participant 61:

> Got bit in the lip by my grandparent's dog and had stitches, but it didn't faze my love for dogs, just for that one.

Six respondents described cleaning up after the pet as being a significantly negative experience typified by this comment from Participant 23,

> "yes, when they throw up and I have to clean it up."

44

Five respondents said their memorable negative experience occurred when their parents got rid of a pet. Participant 73 explains:

> The death of my cats was very hard! My mother gave my dog away when I went to school and I've always hated her for that.

Participant 101 described the following unusual negative incident with her dog,

> "yes, we had a dog that ate the whole kitchen."

These comments revealed that the most negative experience with pets occur when they die. Several (n=26) participants expressed severe negative emotions when losing their pet, whom many considered their best friend. A few respondents (n=11) told the story of being bitten by a dog and other participants (n=6) said they were attacked by a cat. In addition, some respondents (n=6) didn't like cleaning up after their pets and five experienced negative emotions when their pet was given away.

Pet Love

Question 9 asked, "If you have ever felt loved by a pet, if so, in what ways?" Of the 96 participants, only five answered "no" to this question, and only one person avoided answering this question. Of the remaining 90 (93.8%) who said "yes," all shared an experience to support this answer. Participant 24 stated that he has felt loved by a pet because of their,

> "uncomplicated animal ways."

Sixteen respondents reported their pet nuzzled them for attention and was very protective over them in this regard. Participant 67 remarked:

> I have felt loved by my cat because when I was little and upset (crying) he would always come rub against me.

Similarly, Participant 100 replied:

> Of course, they snuggle with me when I'm upset or angry, they always run to the door all happy to see me, and they pout when I go on vacations.

Participant 102 reported:

> Yes, when I'm laying sick on the bed, it's my puppy who comes to cuddle me! Quincy always knows when I need to be alone or not.

Fourteen participants said they knew their pet loved them because every night they would sleep, cuddle, and lick their face. Participant 40 explained,

> "yes! They show affection by sleeping with you or licking."

Participant 39 reported the following "loving" actions of her pet:

> Yes, she would sleep with me at night and purr when I petted her, she even would lick my face.

Fourteen respondents reported they knew their pet(s) loved them because their pet(s) were always happy to have them around, they were their everyday companion. This reaction is epitomized by the following comment from Participant 19:

> Yes, it's hard to explain if you don't have a/or have never had a pet. You can just sense it. They are always so happy when you get home, etc.

Fourteen respondents chronicled their pet(s) as loving them because they were always there when they came home and were lovable in the subsequent interaction. For example, Participant 48 said she knew her cat loved her because,

> "she would sit by the door and wait for me to come home and he only."

Participant 33 attested love from her dog with:

> Yes, I feel my dog loves me because he runs to me when I get home and sleeps in my room.

Fourteen participants said they knew their pet loved them because they would comfort them when they felt sad. For example, Participant 47 commented,

"my cats always laid with me on the couch and comforted me when I cried." Participant 36 agreed:

One dog that I had knew when something was wrong with me and would lay in my lap to comfort me.

Likewise, Participant 54 described the behavior of her cats:

Two of the cats we've had have been especially comforting, my cat now always stayed by my mom during her chemo-aftermath like he knew something was wrong.

These examples explicate substantial love for and from pets and their owners. Several quotations seemed to capture the essence of the love a pet offers an individual and their family. The respondents wrote about the comfort they felt from their pet when they came home, the companion they were able to have when they felt sad and needed to talk, and their pet's need for attention. These were all appreciated, cherished demonstrations of love from pets that was reciprocated by love the participants felt for their pets.

Relationships within the Family

Question 10 asked, "In what ways was the relationship you had with a pet similar or different from any relationships you had with family members?" Of the 96 participants, four answered "no" to this question, and 11 did not answer this question. Of the 81 who answered "yes," 20 said it was better because your pet would not judge your behavior, argue with you, or criticize anything you said. Participant 35 described her pet as being "nonjudgmental of her," and Participant 54 described how you can "spill your guts" with a pet and "they will never tell or argue." The same thing was described by Participant 43 who reported, there is no "bickering, shouting, or misunderstandings" when talking to a pet.

Participant 65 said her relationship with her pet was similar to that with her family with the following:

> Same, because I could talk to her about things and I could talk to my parents-different in that I could tell her things I couldn't tell my parents because she wouldn't repeat what I said.

Participant 91 revealed an insight about why conversations with animals are so valuable:

> You can always talk to animals cause they can't tell your secrets. Growing up, it's nice to be able to do that. I didn't tell my parents or sisters anything.

Participant 85 described her conversations with her pet:

> As strange as it may be, I could talk out loud to my pet who relieved stress, helped me talk out things in my own mind.

Participant 86 agreed when she expressed:

> I can talk to my pets about things going on in my life when I couldn't tell anyone else about relationships with boyfriends and major college choices.

Eleven respondents depicted their relationship with their pet better than the one with their own family, claiming more affection and love with a pet. Participant 87 explained,

> Keiser and I were always together. I liked him better then my family most of the time.

Likewise, Participant 102 reflected:

> I almost believe the relationships with pets can be much more intense than with people. With people you have all these beliefs, feelings, and sometimes bad experiences, but with pets it's all about love all the time.

Nine respondents described their pet as being another family member-- a comfort that was always around and always consistent. Participant 30 described herself as

"always feeling at home when she is around her pets,"

along with Participant 100 who said her animals are

"not nearly as quick to be frustrated with her as her family can be."

Of the 81 participants who answered this question, everyone attached a positive quality about their pet and reflected on how they contributed to their family in pleasant and constructive ways.

The Power of Pets

Question 11 asked, "How have pets helped you feel better about yourself." Of the 96 participants, 10 said their pet had not helped them feel better about themselves and six didn't answer the question. Of the 80 (83.3%) who indicated their pets helped them feel better about themselves, 15 said they did this by providing unconditional love and respect and always facilitating a happy, brighter day.

Participant 102 reported,

"they remind me that I can brighten someone's day by just smiling."

Participant 47 related,

"they make me have brighter days, cheer me up."

Several participants (n=15) talked about the unconditional love a pet provided, as illustrated by this comment from Participant 26,

"they always seem to love you and never judge you."

Similarly, Participant 39 said,

> "by loving me when I felt like everyone else was mad at me."

Ten respondents described their pet as building their "self-esteem," listening to and allowing their problems to be forgotten. For example, Participant 29 claimed:

> They have been friends who will listen to me and my problems. They help build self-esteem and confidence from the relationships we share.

Sixteen respondents talked about their pets helping them feel better about themselves because they focused on them when they were sad, and they showed affection and assurance when needed. Participant 86 remarked that her pets love her when she is having a bad day. This kind of attention from a pet can be extremely important when needing a companion, as reflected in this comment by Participant 51:

> Sometimes when I'm upset I go talk to Abby and Sable and curl up to them- may sound dumb- but it helps.

Similarly, Participant 93 remarked:

> They calm me and ease me from a stressful day, and are always there to listen even though they can't talk back.

These quotations illustrated how a pet can provide a happy medium for an individual. When other people are not available, the pet can relieve loneliness and boredom. A pet can sit there quietly while an individual expresses his or her thoughts and emotions without uttering a harsh word or conflicting reactions. At times people need interpersonal feedback, but often it's sufficient to just have the opportunity to express how one feels.

Family Members

Question 12 asked, "Were the pets in your house considered family members, if so, in what ways?" Of the 96 respondents, 13 (13.5%) said "no" to this question and one did not answer it. Of the 82 (85.4%) participants who did answer "yes" to this question, Participants 17 and 95 both talked about how their pets were actual "family members" because they had a stocking at Christmas time, got gifts on holidays, and had their names signed to holiday cards. Similarly, Participant 30 wrote:

> Yes, our pets are considered family. They get people food, presents, and their own stockings at Christmas.

Participant 63 indicated that members of her family wrote cards to their pets on holidays.

Seventeen (17.7%) respondents said their pets were part of their immediate family and were included in vacations. This was specified by Participant 47:

> Yes, they were allowed to lay on top of the dinner table when we ate, could go anywhere in the house, we took them on car trips, if were sick took care of them.

Five respondents said their pets were considered a sister or brother to the family, as Participant 74 indicated,

> "my dad refers to Molly as my "sister."

Participant 93 confirmed this notion with,

> "They were either like my children, or my brothers/sisters."

Five respondents said their pets ate their "people" food, and at times, "ate better than we did!," as mentioned by Participant 70.

Participant 56 confirmed this sentiment with:

Bingo was an indoor pet. She would go with us to my grandparents' houses. She ate people food. Slept in my bed.

Five participants described their pet as being in the family photographs and greeting cards, as illustrated by the following statement from Participant 97, "we sign our greeting cards with our <u>and</u> their names." Participant 100 supported the notion that pets are family members with:

Yes they are. They receive the same amount of love, care, and attention as my family members, as well as serving their own role within my family's structure.

These quotations provide instructional evidence regarding pets as a family member. Common themes within answers to this question consisted of the popular phrases, "talked to like a person," "member of the family," and even, "one of us."

Summary

The answers to the survey questions were quite diverse, but nearly all supported the power of pets in influencing family relationships. Many claimed pets reduced stress by facilitating laughter and distractions when human interaction got too demanding or negative. Pets were also commonly considered another playmate who stimulated family bonding, which often improved relationships among family members. In addition, many respondents appreciated the consistency of their pets' behavior, especially the special love they expressed in their own way. It was common for pets to be viewed as a person's best friend-- a loyal companion at times when love and attention were most needed.

Pets were also perceived to be a positive listener at times when no person was around, or when those available were emotionally unstable, or when the participant only wanted to share a secret with someone they knew would never repeat it.

Pets also provided protection and comfort, depending upon a person's needs. Some considered their pet the "biggest joy" in life which could boost their self-esteem when they needed it most. Pets supplied assurance, affection, and unconditional love when it seemed to be invisible, unreachable, or distant from family members. The quotations in this chapter are representative samples of numerous others that support the themes reviewed here. Appendix D contains verbatim transcriptions of all responses to the 102 surveys, providing further evidence of the themes.

Chapter Five

Discussion and Conclusions

Overview

This study used a survey with open-ended questions to explore the impact
and importance of a pet on family members, especially how a pet influences the
relationships its caretaker has with other family members. A total of 102 surveys
were distributed to university students, 96 of those students had a pet, and 82
respondents (85.4%) indicated they had a pet who influenced their life in important
ways.

An underlying assumption of this study was that pets provide an important
dynamic for families in that they can decrease stress and anxiety, and provide
personal comfort and security. Using symbolic interaction theory as a guide, this
study was designed to examine how pets are important in family relationships.
Symbolic interaction provides a perspective for understanding the family and other
social worlds. It also offers guidance for understanding communication within a
family, explaining how a pet might be a facilitator of communication, and defining
various roles a pet can play in family life.

In addition to theory, two basic research questions guided this study, and the
data analysis process:

(1) In what ways can a pet influence a person's life regarding family
relationships?

(2) In what ways can a pet replace or act as a beneficial substitute for other
interpersonal, significant relationships?

Discussion

Relationships between the research questions and the responses to the surveys are depicted in Table 5.1. These results are addressed in the sections that follow.

Table 5.1

Relationships between Research Questions and Themes within Survey Answers

Research Questions	Themes
A Pet's influence in a person's family life	Ease stress, another playmate, family bonding, another family member, consistent reactions, unconditional love
Relationship role of family pet(s)	Best friend, listener, protector, comforter, communicator, biggest joy, self-esteem builder, provides security, comfort, and affection

The common themes support the remarkable influence a pet can have on a person's family life, particularly with regard to the significant role that pet plays in relationships between family members and between the pet and individuals in the family. These themes were derived from survey answers and established as consistent and repetitious opinions of participants when discussing their family pet(s).

Research Question 1 asked: "In what ways can a pet influence a person's life regarding family relationships?" They ease stress and reduce conflicts between family members by providing a positive atmosphere and a beneficial distraction. Also, pets often provide another playmate for family members who are always available and consistently affectionate.

Pets can facilitate family bonding and initiate contact between family members by consistently seeking attention and affection. They can provide an active or passive medium for interpersonal conversation, or give people something to talk about. They are often considered another member of the family because of the special companionship they provide.

Most participants expressed how pets, in their own unique ways, give individuals a certain contentment that can strengthen positive forces within the family. Pets are described as serving a valuable role within the family system, including a vehicle for affection, fun, and exercise. They are also a source of emotional security and protection, and they help teach children important caretaking responsibilities and a respect for life.

Pets are perceived as being "consistent" in their actions and in their relationships within the family. Respondents listed their pets as: "keeping the peace," "providing an escape," "nuzzling for attention," "lovable," "consistent," "dependent," "non-authoritative," "building self-esteem," "listening," and "providing brighter days." They willingly hear all problems and all worries that might be causing distress. They are "happy to have you around," and they maintain a friendly countenance that can impact individuals and their interactions with other family members.

Pets also bring unconditional love to the entire family which exemplifies the kind of "actively caring" family members need to show toward each other (Geller, 2001). Thus, pets are perceived as providing an example for the kind of unconditional love that makes families special. There is meaningful communication between an individual and their pet. Respondents expressed their pets as being there to "keep company," "make you happy," and "help you to forget your problems." Whether understood by others, this form of conversation can fulfill a meaning of importance to an individual that is sometimes preferred over interpersonal communication (Klein & White, 1996; LaRossa & Reitzes, 1993).

A questionnaire survey of pet owners (n=53) distributed by Friedmann and Tomas (1985) revealed many of the same themes found in this study. Over 50% of the pet owners in this survey reported they talk to their pets frequently, as if they were people, and considered their pets to be sensitive to their moods (Friedmann & Thomas, 1985). A similar kind of attachment was expressed by the participants in the current study, demonstrating that when in need of close, affectionate contact with others, the family pet can be beneficial. Such relationships with pets can provide invaluable emotional support when people need to cope with physical and psychological stressors in their everyday lives (Brickel, 1985; Serpell, 1996).

Many participants used the survey to project personal and strong feelings about their pets. These reactions to the questions provided instructive information regarding various ways a family pet affected many years of dynamic interpersonal relationships. Such self-disclosure revealed solid evidence of the valuable role pets can play in the development and maintenance of healthy family relationships.

Research Question 2 asked: "In what ways can a pet replace or act as a beneficial substitute for other interpersonal, significant relationships?" The participants described numerous significant relationships with their pets. Through personal anecdotes, respondents depicted their pets as a "best friend"-- providing special companionship that is consistently available whenever needed.

Many pets were described as great listeners who never pass critical judgment, never interrupt, never force opinions upon the individual, and never hold a grudge. Such commentary implies that connecting with a pet is usually simpler and less stressful than building relationships with humans.

Pets are often depicted as protectors, whether they protect the entire family or just a particular individual in that family. They also provide comfort when needed, both actively as an affectionate playmate and passively as a resilient soundingboard for verbal expressions of emotional and/or physical pain.

Pets enable and facilitate interpersonal communication within the family, whether it is "who fed the dog today?" or, "does someone want to walk Bear with me?" Regardless of the type of communication promoted within the family, pets play a pivotal role in everyday family interactions and relationships. Pets can open communication lines. They provide a purpose for interpersonal communication and set the occasion for certain interactions, some implying the sharing or responsibilities.

The reported impact of pets on interpersonal communication within a family is consistent with the results of a study accomplished by Cain (1985). In that study a number of specific instances were described where a pet was used to stabilize a family. When family members were dealing with conflict, the pet might intercede and knowingly do something to distract from the argument.

From the current study, participants indicated that the family pet is often perceived as a tremendous source of joy in their lives. For these people the pet is the one they look forward to seeing when they come home, the one to whom they convey all their problems and worries, and the one they know has unconditional positive regard for them. The pet can boost self-esteem by showing appreciation for simple acts of affection, kindness, and caring. The family pet welcomes and reciprocates unconditional love.

Beck (1999) and Brickel (1985) offer similar conclusions by explaining how a pet can be there for attention and affection when no one else is available; a pet can appear to listen when the rest of the world seems disinterested; a pet can offer unconditional love when love from people seems to be conditional. Moreover, Beck (1999) discusses the special advantages of communicating with a pet, given that the pet does not argue, interrupt, or disagree but rather just sits there and seemingly takes it all in (Beck, 1999). As such, pets become a person's special friend that provides an escape from a seemingly negative, uncaring, or misunderstanding world (Beck, 1999; Brickel, 1985). As many participants in the current study expressed, pets bring love to the family, listen with apparent interest when no one else seems interested, and are loyal unconditionally, unlike many relationships with humans that vary according to conditions and contingencies.

Conclusions

The current research supports and broadens the importance of a pet in building and sustaining meaningful family relationships. Pets do play a variety of roles in a family and these can differ dramatically from individual to individual. Pets were seemingly important to each of the 96 participants who had a pet while they were growing up, as well as the six participants who did not have a pet while they were growing up. Each of these respondents to the survey of 12 open-ended questions offered a story about their own pet that reflected special significance linked to owning a pet. The six participants without pets express positive feelings when in contact with other people's pets and their disappointment on not having their own pet.

For the 102 participants in this survey research, it was evident that pets played an important role in their lives, especially with regard to family interactions and relationship building. Each pet owner sought out and maintained healthy relationships with their pets, and they perceived these relationships as providing emotional and/or physical support. Each respondent perceived special importance in their relationships with their pet both for themselves and for other family members.

The following section examines limitations of the current study. This research, and that preceding this study, has only cracked the surface in reaching an understanding about the value of pets for individual benefit and for cultivating beneficial family relationships. Much more research in this domain is needed.

Limitations of this Study

My personal perspective about pets may be viewed as a source of bias. Being a lover of animals and entangled with pets on a daily basis, I find myself redefining my relationships with my pets almost every day. It is easy to be intrigued with animals. If treated well, they have an uncomplicated, peaceful way of life, and add an important component to daily human life. As such, pets provide an exemplar humans can model when the complexities and conflicts of their lives call for retreat.

Pets can calm human nerves, rest human hearts, and encourage human affection. They are trustworthy animals that seem to have a simple enjoyment of life that escapes the humdrum of much human experience. People often make a simple problem more complex and difficult to resolve, whereas pets just take in what the world offers, without adding biased and stressful interpretation. The results of this study indicate that many people experience this same positive relationship with a pet.

This study offers only a small glimpse of the perceptions of other pet owners with regard to how their pet(s) have influenced their lives. The sample was relatively small and selective. In addition, the sample was not representative of any particular population, but was a convenience sample. In other words, the 102 participants were students in undergraduate university courses. These students are not a representative sample, but were those conveniently sampled from six university courses across two universities in southeastern U.S.

While the opinions and perceptions were quite consistent among the survey respondents, the select nature of the sample limits external validity. In other words, the results have limited generalizability. For example, one might obtain very different perceptions from individuals of different education levels, ages, and social economic status. Clearly, surveys of pet relationships need to be administered to broader audiences.

The literature contains very little exemplars in which to base follow-up research. Most related research articles addressed pets assisting humans with physical limitations, but little research has studied the impact of pets in family relationships. The few studies that did address pets and family relationships provided few details on characteristics of the participants. Thus, the results of the present study cannot be compared with prior research.

Another limitation of the current research was the survey itself. All but one of the questions asked for beneficial experiences with pets. Only one question assessed negative experiences with a pet. As a result, the survey likely set the occasion for more positive than negative reactions regarding pets and their relationships with family members. An objective survey which listed possible negative consequences might have influenced more negative reactions.

In addition, the nature of the survey administration probably limited the amount of reaction to each question. In other words, the survey was administered in a university classroom setting with a minimal time to complete (about 15 minutes). A longer administration time might certainly have resulted in more extensive answers. Individual interviews would no doubt offer more in depth descriptions and personal anecdotes. Along with the option of asking the participant to elaborate on a particular topic which might heighten the interest of the interviewer and offer a more in-depth answer to a question.

Suggestions for Further Research

One direction for further research is to broaden the demographics of the sample. The existing literature in this domain of study is very limited, so assessing reactions from respondents other than college students would add useful information to the knowledge base. Most of the research on pets addresses their use as aids for individuals with certain physical challenges. The role of pets in helping people with emotional challenges has rarely been addressed. This was the purpose of the present exploratory qualitative study. It clearly showed that pets provide emotional security and support to many. But many questions remain, including:

- What age groups are beneficial most by pets and in what ways?
- What kind of pet (e.g., dog vs. cat) has the greatest beneficial impact?
- Do certain people benefit more from one kind of pet versus another?
- What personality characteristics of people (states or traits) are most conducive to obtaining reciprocal benefits from pets?
- What is the benefit/cost ratio of owning vs. losing certain kinds of pets?
- Can animals which are used for food (e.g., cows, pigs) become influential pets?
- What cultural differences (within the U.S. and worldwide) influence what animals are influential pets?

- How does the influence of pets in family relationships vary across cultures within the U.S. and worldwide?

There are only a few of the numerous empirical questions worthy of follow-up investigation. The present research only showed that pets are perceived as valuable entities in a family. Much more systematic study is needed to:

a) determine the generalizability of these findings,

b) define factors that increase versus decrease the benefits of pets in family relationships, and

c) understand the qualities of a pet that gives it therapeutic value in developing and sustaining healthy family relationships.

Using a qualitative approach and receiving story telling narratives were very helpful in understanding the impact a certain pet can bring on an individual and his or her family. This survey did provide many real-life narratives that illustrated the importance of pets to certain individuals. A more in-depth interview process (e.g., individual consultation with more descriptive questions that require more extensive reaction) might be more informative regarding the special impact pets can have on individuals and their family relationships.

Finding out how long a particular pet has been living with a family is another attribute worth addressing in follow-up research. In addition, it might be possible to assess the impact of a long-term pet on different developmental stages of a person's life (e.g., preadolescence vs. adolescence). This could be accomplished by requesting the participants to describe more instances with their pet as they progressed through childhood to adolescence.

Indeed, the present study represents only the tip of an interesting iceberg that needs to be systematically investigated. This research demonstrated the extreme importance of this "iceberg" among a select group of college students. Much more exploratory research is obviously needed in this domain.

Summary

The reactions of 102 participants to a 12-item, open-ended survey indicated that pets serve an invaluable function in family relationships. They can substitute for a significant relationship (i.e., another child) or they can become a playmate that provides unconditional love and emotional security. Respondents indicated that pets contribute to family bonding, bring unconditional love into the family, serve as a person's "best friend," and boost self-esteem. Even the six respondents who did not have a pet while growing up suspected that the presence of a pet might have been beneficial to their needs and the needs of other family members.

In Conclusion

When I first decided to do a study on pets I was struck with the fact that pets have always had a positive influence in my life. They have been helpful, encouraging, peaceful, and comforting. I have always been intrigued with the relationship of one's pet to an individual or a family. In this study, respondents reported a dramatic influence from pets in their lives. They were there when respondents wanted to cry, self-disclose, express anger about a family member, practice their confrontation, or cuddle with before bed. I began this study with the assumption that pets are powerful influential factors in family relationships. This general hypothesis was strongly supported by the data reported here. Most of the respondents commented that pets are "influential," "consistent," "happy to have you around," "an escape," "listeners," "dependent," "lovable," and "always there." These are only some of the positive qualities attributed to pets.

When reading over the surveys, I was astonished by the numerous stories and examples respondents were willing to provide and describe when answering several of the questions. The participants seemed eager to explain how their pets affected "family bonding." Pets were portrayed as being, "the biggest joy in my life," "almost another child," "better than people," "one of the family," "younger brother or sister," "significant relationship," "another playmate," and "more comforting." These comments are representative of the range of perspectives providing confirmation that pets are powerful, influential, important, and loved. If a pet is "powerful," it is powerful for that individual in its own unique way, leaving an exclusive and exceptional impression for that person to understand and embrace.

References

American Veterinary Association (AVMA). (1983). *The veterinary services market, Vols. I & II*. Overland Park, KS: Charles, Charles & Associates.

Anderson, R. S. (Ed.). (1974). *Pet animals and society*. London: Bailliere Tindall.

Barone, M. (1998). The truth about cats and dogs. *Fairfield County Woman, XXX*, 36-39.

Beck, A. B. (1999). Companion animals and their companions: Sharing a strategy for survival. *Technology and Society, 19,* 201-203.

Beck, A. M., & Katcher, A. (1996). *Between pets and people: The importance of animal companionship*. West Lafayette, IN: Purdue University Press.

Beck, A., & Katcher, A. (1983). *Between pets and people: The importance of animal clinician*. New York: G. P. Putnam's Sons.

Bogdan, R. C. & Biklen, S. K. (1998). *Qualitative research in education, an introduction to theory and methods (3rd ed.)*. Needham Heights, MA: Allyn & Bacon.

Boss, P. G., Doherty, W. J., Larossa, R., Schumm, W. R., & Steinmetz, S. K. (Eds.). (1993). *Sourcebook of family theories and methods: A contextual approach*. New York: Plenum.

Brickel, C. M. (1985). Initiation and maintenance of the human-animal bond: Familial roles from a learning perspective. *Pets and the family,* 31-63.

Bridger, H. (1976). The changing role of pets in society. *Journal of Small Animal Practice, 17,* 1-8.

Bruner, J. (1983). Play, thought, and language. *Peabody Journal of Education, 60(3)*, 60-69.

Cain, A. O. (1985). A study of pets in the family system. In A.H. Katcher & A.M. Beck (Eds.). *New perspectives on our lives with companion animals.* Philadephia: University of Pennsylvania Press, 1983.

Cain, A. O. (1985). Pets as family members. In Sussman, M. B. (Ed.). (1985). *Pets and the family* (p. 5-10). New York; Haworth Press.

Davis, J. H., & Juhasz, A. M. (1985). The preadolescent/pet bond and psychosocial development. *Pets and the family*, 79-95.

Eckstein, D. (2000). The pet relationship impact inventory. *The Family Journal: Counseling and Therapy for Couples and Families, 8*, 192-198.

Entin, A. D. (1986). The pet focused family: A systems theory perspective. *Psychotherapy in Private Practice, 4*, 13-17.

Fitzpatrick, M. A. & Ritchie, L. D. (1993). Communication theory and the family. In Boss, P. G., Doherty, W. J., Larossa, R., Schumm, W. R., & Steinmetz, S. K. (Eds.). (1993). *Sourcebook of family theories and methods: A contextual approach* (p. 565-585). New York: Plenum.

Fogle, B. (1983). *Pets and their people.* London: Collins Harvill.

Friedman, E., & Thomas, S.A. (1985). Health benefits of pets for families. In Sussman, M. B. (Ed.). (1985). *Pets and the family* (p. 191-202). New York; Haworth Press.

Gall, M. D., Borg, W. R., & Gall, J. P. (1996). *Educational research: An introduction (6ᵗʰ ed.).* White Plains, NY: Longman.

Geller, E. S. (2001). *Psychology of safety handbook.* Boca Raton, Florida: CRC
Press.

Gergen, K. J. (1999). *An invitation to social construction.* London: Sage.

Katcher, A. H. (1981). Interactions between people and their pets: Form and
function. In B. Fogle (Ed.). *Interactions between people and pets* (pp. 41-
67). Springfield, IL: Charles C. Thomas.

Klein, D. M., & White, J. M. (1996). *Family theories: An introduction.* Gillian
Dickens: Sage.

LaRossa, R., & Reitzes, D. C. (1993). Symbolic Interactionism and Family
Studies. In Boss, P. G., Doherty, W. J., Larossa, R., Schumm, W. R., &
Steinmetz, S. K. (Eds.). (1993). *Sourcebook of family theories and methods:
A contextual approach* (p. 135-163). New York: Plenum.

Larsen, K. S., Ashlock, J., Caroll, C., Foote, S., Feeler, J., Keller, E., Seese, G., &
Watkins, D. (1974). *Laboratory aggression where the victim is a small dog.
Social Behavior and Personality, 2,* 174-176.

Levinson, B. M. (1968). Interpersonal relationships between pet and human being.
In M. W. Fox (Ed.). *Abnormal behavior in animals.* Philadelphia: W. B.
Saunders.

MacDonald, A. J. (1979). Review: Children and companion animals. *Child Care,
Health and Development, 5,* 359-366.

Netting, F. E., Wilson, C. C., & New, J. C. (1987). The human-animal bond:
Implications for practice. *Social Work, 32,* 60-64.

Paul, E. S. (2000). Empathy with animals and with humans: Are they linked? *Anthrozoos, 13,* 194-202.

Roberts, T. W. (1994). Human-pet bonding and family functioning: A systems approach. *Family Science, 7,* 67-77.

Rowan, A. N. (Ed.). (1988). *Animals and people sharing the world.* University Press of New England: Hanover and London.

Sable, P. (1995). Pets, attachment, and well-being across the life cycle. *Social Work, 40,* 334-341.

Serpell, J. (1996). *In the company of animals: A study for human-animal relationships.* Cambridge England; New York.

Soares, C. J. (1985). The companion animal in the context of the family system. In Sussman, M. B. (Ed.). (1985). *Pets and the family* (p. 49-63). New York; Haworth Press.

Spicer, L. (1990). Our furry relations. *The Optimist, 16,* 13-14.

Sussman, M. B. (1985). Pet/human bonding: Applications, conceptual and research issues. *Marriage and Family Review, 8,* 1-3.

Veevers, J. E. (1985). The social meanings of pets: Alternative roles for companion animals. In Sussman, M. B. (Ed.). (1985). *Pets and the family* (p.11-31). New York; Haworth Press.

Appendices

Appendix A

This survey will be on one complete page with room on the back for added

responses.

The following is completely voluntary

1. Did you have a pet(s) while you were growing up?   Yes _____No_____

2. If yes to Question 1, how many and what kind of pet(s) did you have?

_____

_____

3. If no to Question 1, how did not having a pet affect you or your family relationships? (feel free to write more on the back.)

_____

_____

_____

4. How well were pets perceived and treated in your family?

_____

_____

5. Was there a particular pet that was most influential in your life? What kind of pet was it? What was its name? How old were you?_____

_____

6. Did this pet act as a significant relationship in your life, if so, in what ways?_____

_____

7. How have pets affected you and the relationships you had within your family? (i.e., help with communication between family members, cause or help with stress in the family) _____

_____

_____

8. Did you ever have any negative experiences with a pet?_____

_____

_____

9. Have you ever felt loved by a pet? If so, in what ways?_____

_____

_____

_____

10. In what ways was the relationship you had with a pet similar or different from any relationships you had with family members?_____

_____

_____

_____

11. How have pets helped you feel better about yourself?_____

_____

_____

12. Were the pets in your house considered family members, if so, how?_____

_____

_____

What is your Age:_____ & Gender: M_____ F_____

Appendix B

The following is completely voluntary

If you are interested in being contacted for more information about this project and participating in an interview please put your VT email address here:_____

AND place the first two letters of the town/city you were born here:____ ____

AND place the first two letters of your mother's maiden name here: ____ ____

AND place the number of the month in which you were born (e.g., Jan = 01, Dec = 12) here: ____ ___

1. Did you have a pet(s) while you were growing up? Yes____No_____

2. If yes to question 1, how many and what kind of pet(s) did you have?

_____

_____

3. If no to question 1, did not having a pet affect you and your relationships within your family? How? Why? (please feel free to write more on the back of this survey.)_____

_____

_____

_____

4. If yes to question 1, of the pets that you had while growing up, which, if any, was the most influential in your life, what kind of pet was that pet?_____

_____

_____

5. How did that pet affect you and the relationships you had within your family? (e.g., help with communication between family members, help with stress within the family, etc.)_____

_____

_____

6. Did you feel that this pet loved you? Yes_____ No_____ If so, in what ways?_____

_____

7. Did this pet replace a significant relationship in your life? Yes_____ No_____ If so, in what ways?_____

_____

8. How did your personality influence the kind of relationship you had with this pet? (e.g. did this pet calm your nerves, stress you out, make you more relaxed, etc.)_____

_____

_____

9. Did this pet help you to feel better about yourself? Yes___ No___ If so, in what ways?_____

_____

_____

10. Was this pet considered a family member? Yes_____ No____ If so, in what ways?_____

_____

_____

11. Was the relationship you had with your pet similar to any relationships you had with a family member? Yes___

No___ If so, in what ways?_____

_____

_____

24 Males
78 Females
Age:
      19: 9
      20: 28
      21: 42
      22: 18
      23: 3
      24: 2
102 Participants

1. Did you have a pet(s) while you were growing up?
    6 No
    96 Yes

2. If yes to question 1, how many and what kind of pet(s) did you have?
Pets listed: Dogs, cats, kittens, gerbils, hamsters, lizards, guinea pigs, fish, bunnies, anoles, birds, ducks, mice, frogs, donkey's, horses, cows, sheep, turtles, hermit crabs, and pigs.
P1: N/A
P2: N/A
P3: N/A
P4: N/A
P5: N/A
P6: N/A
P7: Black Lab/ Several Lizards
P8: 1 dog, 1 guinea pig, several fish, bunnies, anoles, bird (not all simultaneously)
P9: 4- 2 cats, 2 dogs
P10: 2 cats, 1 dog
P11: 2 dogs, then 1 dog, also, 2 incredibly shy cats
P12: Dog (2)
P13: Ducks, dogs, rabbits, birds
P14: I had a dog, Feather (wire-haired fox-terrier) until 3rd grade, she died. The dog I have now, Scruffy (a terrier mutt) we have had since my freshman year in H.S.
P15: 2, 1 Gold fish, 1 German Shepherd.
P16: 3 dogs, fish, parakeet.
P17: Dog, cats, rabbits, donkey, horse, fish.
P18: 4 dogs, 1 cat, 1 rabbit, (not at same time).
P19: One dog (pepper).
P20: Fish, but they don't count. 2 dogs (not the same time) dachshunds.
P21: dog
P22: 1 dog (maltese)
P23: 2 dogs, 3 cats (not all at same time)
P24: dog

P25: 3 cats, numerous dogs, 3 horses, cows, pigs, etc (we lived on a farm)
P26: 2 cats, 1 dog
P27: Two cats and a dog
P28: 1 dog, 1 guinea pig (2)
P29: over 200- sheep, cats, dogs
P30: 5 dogs, 3 cats, fish
P31: I had so many, I don't remember, I do know, though, that they were all cats.
P32: dogs, 3-4 dogs, cats 1-2
P33: I had several cats and one dog and guinea pig
P34: 3 dogs, 4 cats-kittens (numerous) 1 hamster, 1 bird.
P35: 1 dog
P36: Eight and they were all mixed breeds
P37: 1 cat-died, 3 dogs-two are now dead
P38: 1 dog, 3 cats (different times), lots of hamsters
P39: one cat
P40: 2 dogs and cats- lots over time!!
P41: 3 dogs; 1 cat; 4 gerbils; 1 guinea pig; 1 goldfish
P42: German shepherd (2) Golden retriever (1) Black lab (1) Porter collie (1)
P43: goldfish- 3
P44: 1 dog and 1 cat
P45: I had one dog
P46: 3 cats and 1 dog
P47: 8 turtles, 1 dog, 2 cats
P48: I had one cat
P49: One dog
P50: Black lab when I was really little, yellow lab since I was nine, had a few mice, fish guinea pig along the way
P51: I've had 4 cats, 3 hamsters, some fish, a lizard, and a frog—oh! And 1 bunny rabbit
P52: 1 cat – occasionally fish, 1 dog
P53: 1 cocker spaniel dog, 4-5 cats, 1 German shepherd, 1 mutt dog 'Rose'
P54: 3 cats (not at the same time 1 then 2), turtle, rabbits
P55: 2 poodles until age 7-8. An adopted 4 cats, hasa opso mix, from age 9-present. 2 outdoor lab mixes. Fish, an iguana, quacker parrot.
P56: I had one female dog, Bingo
P57: Dog, total of 8, 1 cat, most recent- smokey, my puppy yorkie-poo
P58: 5 dogs, 2 cats, 1 hamster, 1 parrot
P59: CATS!!! Lots of them – 6 was the most, but there was always at least 1 or 2 that we spoiled a lot – a sort of "favorite"
P60: We had three cats growing up – but only one at a time. (Patches, Pepper, & Nora)
P61: dogs, (5 different ones), birds, fish
P62: 4 or so cats, 3 hamsters and more frogs and lizards then I can possibly count
P63: hamsters (3); dog (1); outside cats (2)
P64: one cat – every time the cat would pass away we would get another one
P65: I had a cat and then a dog

P66: Always one pet dog and then a handful of beagles, that we, my dads hunting dogs, also various cats, fish, hamsters, frogs

P67: 2 cats

P68: Fish, pony, 3 cats

P69: I had a dog and a cat

P70: 1 dog

P71: dogs (3)

P72: Depended on the time- usually 2 dogs, sometimes 1 or 3 we also had a pot-bellied pig for a while and we raised a baby squirrel

P73: Age 2-12 we had cats. Two. Age 14-18 dog, huskey/shepherd mix

P74: 3 hamsters, 10+ fish, 2 dogs, 2 hermit crabs

P75: I had fish, I have had lots of experiences with dogs though

P76: total of 8, now 2 cats (gave 2 away for 1 yr each) 1 dog, had 3 salt water fish (gave away)

P77: Frogs, fish, dog

P78: fish(1), hermit crabs (2/3), hamsters (3), frogs (several at once), dogs (2), cats (6).

P79: 14 dogs, cats and birds

P80: 2 dogs

P81: several dogs and cats but at different time periods

P82: cats-4 dogs-3

P83: Fish (4), frog, hamsters, dog (2), cat, bird (2)

P84: We have 2 dogs now, but we have had a turtle, multiple fish, and 6 other dogs. (Also-1 rabbit, 3 guinea pigs)

P85: 1 dog and several cats (3), 2 hermit crabs

P86: 7 cats, 2 hamsters, 8 fish, 3 dogs

P87: I had 1 dog named kieser, 2 cats- Hannah and gracie and others

P88: 5 cats 3 dogs, 1 hermit crab, 4 hamsters, 10 fish, 1 guinea pig (not all at one time)

P89: 1 dog & 3 hamsters at different times

P90: We had one dog, later when she passed away we got 2 more dogs. In college I have a fish and guinea pig

P91: 2 rabbits, 3 cats, 5 fish, 2 birds

P92: cats, dogs, iguana, fish

P93: 7-cats, 6-gerbils, 3-hermit crabs, goldfish, 1 bird

P94: 2 dogs, 1 turtle, 2 birds, 1 bunny, 1 guinea pig

P95: 2 dogs, 4 guinea pigs, 1 rabbit, 2 cats, 3 hamsters (throughout childhood)

P96: 2 cats and 1 dog

P97: 4, 3 dogs and 1 cat (all Labradors)

P98: 1 cat

P99: 1 mutt, 2 golden retrievers, a rabbit, 2 iguana, 2 silky terriers (all at different times)

P100: 2 dogs, 3 guinea pigs, 1 turtle, mice, now I have my own 2 cats and a dog

P101: Total, 4 dogs, 2 cats, 4 birds, 2 hamsters

P102: 7 cats and 4 dogs

3. If no to question 1, how did not having a pet affect you or your family relationships? (feel free to write more on the back.)

P1: I don't think it affected them at all.

P2: I have no idea.

P3: I always wanted a pet growing up, but mom kept saying no. I think I am still a little upset by her refusal to even consider having one.

P4: I always wanted a pet, but my parents had 9 kids and pets were not allowed. I would have friends with animals and I would play with them often. I never understood why my dad hated dogs, but I didn't really push the issue either.

P5: I think that having a pet in the family adds a sense of unity to a family since they share in one common task-I think my family would have been more relaxed in general if we had had a pet.

P6: I don't know how it affected my family relationships. I don't think I like pets. I am scared of dogs, I guess if we had pets I wouldn't be scared to touch animals.

P7-P24: N/A

P25: It made us more cohesive through interactions with our pets.

P26-P102: N/A

4. How well were pets perceived and treated in your family?

P1: N/A

P2: N/A

P3: We enjoyed pets, my grandfather had two dogs (one died from old age, got another one) lived for 5 years killed by car), my mom just said she didn't want one because we lived in the city. In reality we lived in the suburbs with a large backyard. I just think they were lazy or cheap.

P4: My dad didn't like animals-he saw them as expensive and dangerous. All my siblings love animals and now that we're older-we have our own pets.

P5: They were treated well in our family, but were perceived as causing extra mess and unnecessary money.

P6: We never had one.

P7: Like one of the family.

P8: Perceived and treated as regular family members….I guess.

P9: Sometimes they were perceived as being a hassle, but they were treated well.

P10: Very well, they did live outdoors though.

P11: Pretty much like younger brother/sister, almost.

P12: Very well.

P13: Very well.

P14: Very well. Treated as almost a member of the family. Scruffy has frequented a certain chair (a lazy boy) so often that it has become "his chair"

P15: The German Shepherd was much better received than the goldfish, but both were well received.

P16: Treated well, should have been treated better at times.

P17: Very well.

P18: They were all treated very well

P19: Better than the people, sometimes! ☺

P20: My mom loved our dog, part of the family, relatively.

P21: Very well.

P22: Very well-almost absolutely spoiled.
P23: Perceived and treated well. Shown attention.
P24: Good.
P25: Extremely well.
P26: Very well.
P27: Better than me at some times.
P28: Very well, like another family member.
P29: Extremely well-like members of our family.
P30: Our pets are and have always been treated well in my family.
P31: My mom, sister, and I loved them, but my dad didn't like cats. He did not treat them badly, though.
P32: Fairly well, taken good care of but most stayed outside.
P33: The cats were well liked but my mom hates the dog.
P34: Pets were treated as family members- slept in our beds, on sofa watching T.V., went on trips.
P35: Everyone loved my dog. My dad disciplined her-but only to teach her, occurred when I was young and didn't understand.
P36: They were treated very well and were considered part of the family.
P37: Great, very loved
P38: My family treats our animals as part of the family
P39: They were treated like part of the family
P40: Really well-we love pets!
P41: We loved our pets! We treated them just like they were part of the family.
P42: Family dog, liked and loved.
P43: We loved them. Feeding them and caring for them was a family ordeal. We even said "grace" before we sprinkled the fish flakes into their bowl
P44: As if they were part of the family.
P45: My dog was treated very well and was well liked in my family.
P46: As part of the family.
P47: Very well like they were a family member.
P48: They were treated like family.
P49: Very well, like one of the family.
P50: Treated very well, they were looked at like part of the family.
P51: We loved and cared for them and still do (we still have 2 of our cats). The cats have been disciplined which sometimes includes "hitting"
P52: Everyone loved our dog, my mom loved the cat, my dad and I did not.
P53: Very well- perceived as a responsibility and also a great comfort-something to focus on/talk about-something to share.
P54: Our pets, especially our cats were/are members of our family. When our 1st cat was hit by a car it was a devastating experience. We now have 2 more and they aren't allowed out because of what happened to our 1st.
P55: Treated very kindly and gently by everyone except my younger brother (he was /15 too aggressive with dogs)
P56: We treated Bingo as if she was a part of the family. She was definitely my best friend. She always slept with me. My family gave her unconditional love.
P57: Good- a form of companionship, family bonding.

P58: Pets were treated very well in my family. They were generally the center of attention and were always taken care of.

P59: Well…except for my dad wouldn't allow the cats to stay inside overnight—so we had to put them out—but he and my brother built several "cat houses" for them to stay warm in the winter.

P60: Pets were treated as another member of the family and were perceivable as soft cuddly creatures to be loved.

P61: Perceived as fun and well. Treated well except when one of them got beat by my dad.

P62: Treated very well, spoiled, not the frogs or lizards though, they weren't spoiled.

P63: Great…always given love and affection, treated well (many long walks and treats), lived in a nice house (except cats that hated it inside).

P64: They were treated like one of the family (a child to my parents and a brother/sister to me and my sister)

P65: They were treated as part of our family, almost as another child.

P66: Good-but the dogs and cats never or rarely came inside. They were/are 'pets' not really part of the family.

P67: Perceived well in the beginning, more neglected and perceived as a pain later.

P68: Fish weren't really thought of, they were just there. Pony and cats were loved members of the family.

P69: They were treated well often like family members they have a stocking at Christmas

P70: Excellent, we treated her like another part of the family.

P71: Pets were just like other family member just more lovable and goofy-always there to pet and love and to be loved.

P72: At first, our dogs were for hunting, but then we would get dogs just for pets-they were treated well-given lost of love, but not too spoiled.

P73: My mother hated cats and thought of them as pretty stupid and opinioned animals. To me, they were just another play thing.

P74: The dogs are paid the most attention to, most likely because they are the most active and attention-needy.

P75: Very nicely, always fed and cleaned and given an excellent habitat.

P76: Very well, we love animals, they are part of the family.

P77: The pets were treated very well in my family.

P78: My dad grew up on a farm where cats were pests so he never liked them. Our cat that lived 13 years grew on him though. Everyone else loved them.

P79: Like family members

P80: Very well, like one of the family

P81: Very well until my mom got tired of taking care of it and gave it away

P82: Treated fairly and were close with family members

P83: Very well, it was hard to get a dog though because my mom did not want one, but she loves our dog now.

P84: Pets are so babied by my entire family.

P85: Were treated as family members.

P86: The pets were and still are treated like a member of the family.

P87: Very well, they are treated like a member of our family.

P88: They were treated like a member of the family, and mourned as so when they died.

P89: Treated very well.

P90: Pets were considered to be as part of the family as anyone else-we always treated them the best we could.

P91: Very well, they had a lot of freedom because we live way out in the country and there is a lot of land.

P92: Well

P93: They were treated well and were like my parents children.

P94: They were part of our family, they even received presents on special holidays.

P95: They were perceived as family members and were treated very, very well.

P96: Loved in the home but not brought outside that much.

P97: Very well-treated just like another family member.

P98: She was treated well by everyone

P99: Quite well, my dad likes to make fun of the silky terrier, but treats it like gold

P100: Very well, they are family members and they are spoiled rotten

P101: Depends on how they acted normally, like they are part of the family, but we had a few crazy dogs and we had to get rid of them.

P102: Like kings ☺ they're treated just like one of the family! If I got eggs, they got eggs.

5. Was there a particular pet that was most influential in your life? What kind of pet was it? How old were you?

P1: N/A

P2: No

P3: Yes, I got a pet after my first year in college, a cat named Scooter.

P4: My best friend when I was 11 had a black lab named Sam. We played with Sam everyday. We were there when she had puppies and tried to convince my parents to adopt one. My ex boyfriend in high school had cats and we'd play with them often.

P5: 2 dog-Sparky and Chrissy (ages 3 months-5 years)

P6: No

P7: No

P8: My anole, when I was 8-10, don't remember the name.

P9: Not really.

P10: A dog, husky, I think this was because it was when I was young, name, Smokey.

P11: Yes-Star, a yellow lab, we got her when I was around 10, she was extraordinarily hyper, even for a lab....

P12: Dog, Dusty, 6 and under.

P13: Not really, they just kept me company.

P14: Scruffy, during my teenage years.

P15: The German Shepherd, her name was Virna, I don't remember how old I was when we got her but I was 19 when she died.

P16: Tasha, mixed breed dog, 9.

P17: Dog, Dixie, I was 17.

P18: Influential may be too strong, my most loved pet was a sheepdog named Amber, we had her when in 1-12th grades.

P19: "Pepper"-dog, I was 0-15 years old.

P20: No

P21: No, not really

P22: No

P23: Oldest cat, Maggie, less than 8 years old.

P24: Buddy

P25: Yes-Pit bull (nice, loving, small-not the mean ones always depicted on TV) Jinx, 14.

P26: No

P27: My dog, we've had her for about ten years.

P28: Dog, Andy, part terrier/half poodle, I was seven years old.

P29: Yes, a sheep-Suffolk ewe named 70. 3 years old.

P30: When I was in the first grade, my dad gave me a Bassett hound puppy. Her name was little one.

P31: Yes, Rudy is his name. I got him for my 20th birthday.

P32: Yes- Pomeranian, Killer, got him when I was about 7. He died when I was 20.

P33: I really like my dog the most. It is a cocker spaniel named midnight. I was 15.

P34: N/A

P35: My dog was influential, we adopted her when I was ten years old (11 years ago).

P36: Yes, I got a Jack Russell Terrier last Feb. and he is the biggest joy of my life.

P37: Dog-Tara, Golden retriever, I was about 6-14 years old when she was alive.

P38: Not really influential but extremely important, cat (Rinky Dink), 9 years old-present.

P39: My cat that I got when I was five years old. Her name was Puss (I know that's bad, but I was young).

P40: Boots- cat, I was 7.

P41: My dog Maggie. She's a Yorkshire terrier and I got her for my 16th birthday. I'm her mommy!

P42: German Sheppard #2, Kico, got when I was 15.

P43: Yes, my beta fish, I loved it because it looked like a rainbow. I got it when I was 8, and it died when I was 14.

P44: Yes, a dog that was a mixed breed. I was 10 years old.

P45: Yes, it was my dog, Kody. We got him when I was in 5th grade and he passed away this past Thanksgiving.

P46: My dog Rascal, ½ Pomeranian, ½ sheltie, 8 years now (20yrs).

P47: Yes, my cats, there names were Cuddles and Calie.

P48: This was my family cat that I had growing up. Its name was Pepper and I had him from the time I was 6, when I got him and he died when I was 20.

P49: Dog, Cricket, I was 9.

P50: My dog Travis, we've had since I was nine.

P51: Yes- Daisy, the 1st cat we had, we had Daisy from the time I was born and he died while I was in 4th grade.

P52: My dog Ginger, it was a mix with golden retriever. I was about 7-8.

P53: Eve-German Shepherd- 20 years old.

P54: My 1st cat. Black paws followed my mom and sister home from dropping me off at the bus stop, 1st day of 2nd grade. He was hit my junior year of high school. I felt like I lost a good friend.

P55: Truffles is our ~12 year old Lhasa mix we got from the pound and she's been around for more than ½ my life.

P56: Yes, Bingo, Dog. I was 4 years old when I got her from the Humane society.

P57: Bojangles (aged 5-20) he was a toy poodle.

P58: My dog Ginger, we had her from when I was 7 until 3 weeks ago when she died, so she was basically always around for everything.

P59: Yes- my cat Kelsey- she is now old---12! She was never liked by the other cats- I'm her only true friend- we're like sisters! We got her when I was 10.

P60: Nora-a mackerel tabby (cat) I was ten years old when she died of feline leukemia-she was such a good cat. We put her to sleep in my arms.

P61: First dog, Cotton, listened well, well-behaved, never barked, would always come when you called her, I was 6?

P62: Mt first pet, a hamster named Kimmy, I got her when I was 8.

P63: The dog I have now because he's mine and it's like taking care of my own child. Chance is 2 years old and I got him when I was 20 years old.

P64: Yes-Mark-cat- elementary school.

P65: Yes, she was a Pekinese and Chihuahua dog named Dutchess, I was 3 when we got her.

P66: My dog now, we got him when I was ~13, Calvin a mutt.

P67: Not really-my great grandmothers Collie with cataracts used to freak me out.

P68: My cat Nosey, we got the cats when I was about 7.

P69: My cat mittens, I got him when I was 13.

P70: Dog, Penny, Dachshund, I was in 5th grade.

P71: My dog-Rocco, I was 11 or 12, I think.

P72: Growing up- Mosby, who was a dog. I was about 7-10 years old.

P73: Mysti was my black and white cat and she used to always sleep with me and when I was sad she'd curl up on my lap. Pury was my long haired orange cat, named because he was always purring. Very lazy, very dumb, for a cat he had terrible depth perception and balance. He was our "fat cat." Babe was my dog, we got her after my father died and she and I would spend hours out in the woods. She was pretty wild and defiant (we said she was probably part wolf) but if I ever left home she'd mope and cry and lay down on my bed and stop eating for several days. It was a battle to even get her outside when I was away.

P74: My first dog, a Beagle, when I was 13. His name is Buster. I also cherish our new dog, Molly, a lab.

P75: N/A

P76: Flakey, a cat, I was 15.

P77: No, only had the dog a short time when I was very young. I was attached to my frogs, but they were not influential in my life.

P78: When I graduated from 8th grade I got a kitten to replace the one that had died a few months earlier. Its name was Tuffy.

P79: Yes, my dog now, Zoe, a Chihuahua. I treat her like a child. My first real responsibility for something else.

P80: Yes, dog, chestnut, 7 months-15 years

P81: Yes, my cat named Baby. He is 1 ½ years old and I am 23.

P82: Yes, while I was in Elementary and middle school, cat named KiKi.

P83: My first dog when I was in elementary school. Sniffy, we had to give her away and it was very hard.

P84: My dogs now are most influential. Rumsey is 13 and an irish setter/golden retriever, Halley is 3 and a cocker spaniel.

P85: A cat named Charlie. Middle school-early college years.

P86: A Dog named Dumbo, age 5-20.

P87: My dog Kieser. He was a great dog. The sweetest and cutest. I had him since I was 8.

P88: Bubbles my cat that I had from age 6 till 15, she was my favorite.

P89: Our dog, her name was Bear. I was about 13 years old.

P90: No, all of my pets in my life have been important.

P91: My cat, I watched her being born, her name is Nestle and I was in 7th grade when she was born.

P92: Iguana (Lizard) name-link, 17 years.

P93: Maury, an orange tabby cat, I was around 10 years.

P94: Yes, my bunny named Toffee, he was living from the time I was 7 to 16.

P95: Yes, my cat Hugs, I was 16.

P96: Dog named Mel, age 10, Black lab.

P97: Madonna, yellow lab. I was around 5 when we got her and she's still around ☺

P98: N/A

P99: My 1st golden retriever "Buttons." She came from a top breeder and I was 11 years old. She ended up having a temperament problem and bit people.

P100: No, I have loved and learned from all of them.

P101: No

P102: Yes, my shiatsu puppy, Quincy-when I was 18 years old.

6. Did this pet act as a significant relationship in your life, if so, in what ways?

P1: N/A

P2: N/A

P3: Yes, I think it made my life much happier and acted as a greater connector between my girlfriend and I.

P4: When my best friend moved I missed Sam and when I broke up with my boyfriend I missed his cats, but didn't really influence me otherwise.

P5: These pets were my babysitters and were my play buddies when I was a child.

P6: N/A

P7: N/A

P8: No

P9: N/A

P10: No

P11: Dunno

P12: Yes, spend lot of time with it, upset when it died.

P13: No

P14: Showed me love. Brought me joy, happiness.

P15: Difficult to say exactly, but she was a significant relationship.

P16: Yes, she was my companion, she looked out for me.

P17: Yes, it was a gift to me and my responsibility.

P18: I don't think so.

P19: Yes, always "there" for me to cheer me up.

P20: No

P21: As a friend.

P22: N/A

P23: Not really, kind of first pet, 2 dogs died early in my life about 4-5 or so.

P24: N/A

P25: Yeah, she was my protector and my best friend when at home because I didn't have siblings.

P26: No

P27: She is like my sister

P28: Not really, just a pet to play with, take for walks, and bring to our athletic events.

P29: Yes, as a baby in the field I went up to her and she let me pet her, my parents have a picture of this, it means a lot to me.

P30: Little one was my very first pet of my own. It gave me someone to play with when I got home in the afternoon.

P31: He was a god-send because I had just broken up with my boyfriend of 2 years, and Rudy filled that void for me.

P32: Yes, he was just always there.

P33: This pet was part of a relationship so I think it was a relationship.

P34: No, not really.

P35: She was always there when I was sad-I'd pet her and she'd lay next to me.

P36: He is my buddy.

P37: Good companion.

P38: Yes, she always was there for me, when I was sad, wanted to play, etc. She knows how I am feeling.

P39: Yes, she was comforting when I was upset and kept me company because I was an only child.

P40: Yes, he was my cat! He was stenciled around my room.

P41: I play a big role in her life when she was younger so she tends to come to me most. She sits at my door waiting for me when I'm at college.

P42: Loved and cared for them.

P43: No, it couldn't really communicate with us. Rather, the relationship was within the family.

P44: She was my dog and I raised her from the minute I got her. She was always protective of me and my best friend.

P45: Yes, he was very protective and I felt secure every time he was around.

P46: Yes, he is very special to our whole family, but he is particularly my buddy!

P47: Yes, they always followed me around, were like a friend since I was an only child.

P48: Yes, he was like family.

P49: Yes, because when I moved she was my best friend.

P50: Yes, I loved to pieces with him when I was little, still hug him when I'm sad and love to take him for walks, I love him.

P51: Yes- taught me how to treat an animal. Daisy was so loving and affectionate. A very rare cat! So special to our whole family.

P52: Yes, I use to play with her a lot, she would always try to protect me.

P53: Yes, companion, guardian, entertainment, conversation topic, comfort.

P54: He would always lay on the bed with me, I could even use him as a pillow. He seemed to follow me when I was upset and would sit while I cried, he was a comfort to me through childhood.

P55: Yes, companionship, sweet, I spent a lot of time caring for her. She laid with my mom in bed for 4 years while she was sick.

P56: Bingo was definitely my best friend. I would talk to her when I had a problem, and she always looked at me as if she understood.

P57: He grew up with me. As I got older I began to neglect him-but he was my buddy for 15 years.

P58: Yes, as I said before, she was there during all of the real "milestones" in my family.

P59: She is a great friend….even though we can't talk to each other-I can tell she appreciates me…I'm her caretaker…she was abandoned as a kitten…she is also a great listener.

P60: Nora was always there for me-she always seemed to know when I was upset and I frequently cuddled with her after school.

P61: She was my buddy, a playmate and something to love.

P62: Yes, I loved her, played with her, took care of her and was very upset when she died. We had a funeral.

P63: Yes, he's like my kid so I spoil him and take him everywhere I got if I can; he's always there to talk too ☺

P64: I was really young when we had him, and really young when he died, so I only remember bits and pieces of him.

P65: She was someone I could come home from school and play with. She was always around.

P66: He always greeted me when I got off the school bus.

P67: No

P68: Yes, he was my favorite, we had a bond, he was super affectionate with me.

P69: I would always play with him, pet him, talk to him.

P70: I always went to her crying, held her when lonely.

P71: Yes, pretty significant-I used to play with it and cuddle with the dog when I was sad.

P72: Kind of-he was very lovely and always wanted my attention.

P73: Babe- my dog was my baby. I loved her to death and she depended on me.

P74: I feel Buster brought our family together as a whole, not necessarily just significant to me.
P75: N/A
P76: Flakey was my baby, I had her for a little over a year and had to give her away when I moved to England, she did everything with me; ate, slept, cleaned! She would wait for me to come home and followed me around everywhere.
P77: No
P78: This pet was my very own and he knew it, the family did, and so did I. He was the most loveable animal and every one told me so.
P79: Kept me company with I was sad about losing a friend.
P80: N/A
P81: Yes, I went through a tough time in my life not to long ago. Being able to focus my attention on him helped me tremendously.
P82: Just fun loving, never gave us problems and she would always run to me when I cried.
P83: Yes, I had begged for a dog forever and I found a stray.
P84: They are my babies. They are spoiled rotten because I know they will never hurt me.
P85: Was a friend- relieved stress.
P86: Yes, he was my best friend when I was little.
P87: Yes, Keiser was like one of my best friends.
P88: Yes, they acted like they understood the trouble that went on in my life.
P89: Yes, I always played with her, took her for walks, talked to her and treated and loved her like the rest of my family.
P90: Yes, I have always had a good relationship with my pets. I love to spend time with them- such as playing, walking, and talking with them.
P91: Yes, she would always sleep on my bed when we let her in the house, she was good to talk to when I needed too.
P92: Best friend, used to sleep under pillow at night.
P93: Yes, he was always there to meet me when I got off the bus, and was there when I cried, he knew when I was upset.
P94: Yes, he was my buddy and someone I could cry to when I was young.
P95: Yes, he was my cat, kept me company, cuddled with me, etc.
P96: Very playful, had a great relationship with dog and it was enthusiastic.
P97: I was an only child, she is/was very much a companion.
P98: N/A
P99: She and I would do dog training together-not as significant a relationship between us as is between some other owners and their dogs.
P100: N/A see above answer-(no, I have loved and learned from all of them)
P101: N/A
P102: Yes, he was and still is my confidence, the one I turn to when I want to talk.

7. How have pets affected you and the relationship you had within your family? (i.e., help with communication between family members, cause or help with stress in the family.)

P1: N/A

P2: N/A

P3: Reduced my stress levels, caused some tension when my girlfriend had to move away to nursing school, some discussion as to who would take kitty, she won.

P4: Only caused stress and resentment that we couldn't have one.

P5: No pets.

P6: N/A

P7: The dog we had when I was younger was just like another playmate.

P8: You could say it helped communication, i.e. "who fed the dog?"

P9: They do seem to ease stress.

P10: Haven't

P11: Gives us something to talk about, etc....the lab increases stress because she's so reckless and hyper.

P12: They helped communication, good conversation starter, something to laugh at.

P13: No

P14: Bring comfort, friendliness, and love to our family.

P15: I don't think pets have affected inter-family relationships in my family, at least not from my perspective.

P16: Helps with stress (especially fish).

P17: Caused some stress when it comes to feeding, care etc......

P18: No, my family was always close.

P19: Help with stress, learn responsibility, learn to have other creatures besides humans.

P20: Causes stress when the dog is barking through the night.

P21: Not much.

P22: Somewhat brought us closer together.

P23: N/A

P24: Didn't.

P25: Reduce stress.

P26: Good way to talk to someone about your problems.

P27: They helped with communication.

P28: Served as a stress relief, often did funny tricks and needed to go for walks.

P29: My pets have been members of my family. When I am in Radford at school my cat Gizmo gets depressed, sneaks in my room, and waits for me by the door.

P30: My mom ends up taking care of the pets no matter whose pets they are.

P31: They have always been something that we all cared about and a good source of humor.

P32: Not in any way really.

P33: I think the dog has helped with stress, but it has also caused some stress as well.

P34: Never cause stress just happy times.

P35: My dog added stress between my dad and me and my sister, because he would discipline her as a puppy and we would get angry at him for it.

P36: They help to relieve stress and help you stay in shape.

P37: Help with stress because we can get away from things by going on walks with them.

P38: Relieve stress, someone to keep us company, affection.

P39: It helped with stress.

P40: Helped communication.

P41: I think our pets have brought us closer together. They also teach responsibility to young children.

P42: Topic to talk about.

P43: The pets helped us keep the peace. The shared responsibility and affection were a bonding point for all of us.

P44: Helped ease stress, helped us have fun.

P45: No, our dog was a big part of our life but it didn't affect any of our relationships.

P46: Helped build strong ties by everyone having a chore to do around the house to take care of ourselves and our pets.

P47: Yes, have been there for us when we are relieving stress.

P48: N/A

P49: They know when you're sad because they just sit there and put their head on your lap.

P50: Think they help with communication, give you something to talk about, reduce stress and tension.

P51: Often a source of stress because of clawing furniture, throwing up hair balls a lot. The bunny was so stressful we gave her to a farm. Other than that, the cats have provided comfort and love.

P52: Our dog was like a member of our family, she would unite us, we all shared in love-go on trips, etc.

P53: A cat named T-Kitty was always a source of stress between me and mom. So-So has been a common bond type animal for me and mom.

P54: I think our pets serve as a common ground-we are all pretty different in our house but everyone cares about the pets!

P55: Help with stress, provide a happy medium.

P56: Bingo definitely helped with stress. She was always willing to play. My dad would hit golf balls and she would chase them and bring them back.

P57: Playing with the pets gives us something to bond over. We can talk, walks, etc.

P58: My pets usually helped with stress because you can play with them when you're angry with everyone else.

P59: They're just great to have around- sort of like having kids in the house now that my brother and I are in our 20's and away from home- my parents enjoy them more now.

P60: The cats served as buffers to family stressors and helped facilitate communication when nothing else could be said between members.

P61: Communication, and when the dogs passed, my parents helping me through it.

P62: No real change except it was an outlet for communication, but we would have talked anyway.

P63: Has increased the bond because my parents love Chance just as much as me and have no problem caring for him if something comes up with me, nothing negative.

P64: None

P65: Always gave us something to talk about-what Dutchess had done that day-both good and bad things

P66: Not really

P67: Increased moms stress levels since she is primary caregiver, decreased father's comfort level since he found out he is allergic to cats.

P68: They eventually caused stress because they started urinating on things like couches and rugs.

P69: I think it has helped, everyone loves our cat, even my nieces and nephew.

P70: In between, helped with problem solving, group interaction and cooperation

P71: Not really

P72: No- not really, grieving over them when they died brought us together.

P73: An escape, "I'm going to walk the dog." I'd be gone for as long as I needed, Babe came everywhere with me.

P74: Brought us together as something that is part of all of us.

P75: I believe that pets are generally a lot of work and require lots of time, but the majority of the time I feel they spark conversation, make people move active and friendly.

P76: The animals have always helped us with stress. They provide someone we can talk to about anything.

P77: They have not affected or helped the relationship with my family.

P78: Pets have always been a stress reliever, especially in emotional times.

P79: They have been stress relievers.

P80: N/A

P81: Most pets cause stress in my family.

P82: Problem causes tension when someone's favorite pet does something annoying, but for the most part neutral.

P83: Great because they were part of the family.

P84: Stress a little with who walks them when and who does what to take care of them.

P85: Can bring laughter to any situation, having them around can relieve stress/anger.

P86: The pets are sometimes a cause of worry when they are sick, but for the most part they have brought our family closer together.

P87: Everything was the same. When Keiser died my senior year it was the saddest day. My mom and I have been closer since.

P88: They help with stress, are a big part of the family.

P89: N/A

P90: Our pets helped with family time and helped my family to make decisions.

P91: They are just kinda there occasionally it's an argument when we would let the cats in the house cause my mom didn't like that.

P92: Sometimes can cause stress, mostly helps with happiness.

P93: Helped with stress, eased and calmed us, we all would cater to our pets, they brought the family closer.
P94: Sometimes they did cause fights, about responsibility and stress about everyday activities.
P95: They helped us as children learn responsibility, we had to communicate to our parents the responsibilities we would take on before we were allowed to get the pet.
P96: Allowed for play with the pets as times.
P97: In some cases, help (do things together with dogs); in some cases, stress (responsibilities, etc)- but, these things are family-caused, not dog-caused.
P98: Sometimes she was a comic relief.
P99: Toby, our current silky terrier, provides us with laughs and is always a friend when you are sick.
P100: They are a definite stress release when things get tense, just petting them relaxes the situation.
P101: Help with stress in the family.
P102: To keep up with the responsibilities of taking care of them. We've had to all learn to communicate and work together.

8. Did you ever have any negative experiences with a pet?
P1: I've been chased by dogs.
P2: N/A
P3: Yes, cleaning up the litter box, dealing with puke on a regular basis.
P4: My little sister was bitten by a mean dog on our street.
P5: Had a dog run after me when I was little, at the time I was scared out of my mind- but I still love dogs.
P6: N/A
P7: No
P8: When they died, as they inevitably did, that was pretty negative.
P9: No
P10: I have been bitten by a dog pretty badly, but it wasn't my pet.
P11: Mainly house training.
P12: A dog bit me.
P13: Yes, it died while I was taking care of it.
P14: No.
P15: Yes, none were very negative.
P16: I got bit by a Dalmatian once.
P17: No, except when they die.
P18: No.
P19: When it died. When I "lost" him once in the neighborhood. Vomit/urinated/defecated in the house.
P20: Yes, when she died.
P21: No
P22: No
P23: Yes, when they throw up and I have to clean it up.
P24: No
P25: Yes- when Jinx died.

P26: Got attacked by my cat.

P27: Yes, when my parents got rid of my cats.

P28: No.

P29: No- only with someone else's dogs. Dog attacked me.

P30: No

P31: They used to all get eaten by dogs when I was little.

P32: Just when they died.

P33: The dog refused to be trained. The guinea pigs died from heat which was bad.

P34: No

P35: Another dog attacked mine and it was very traumatic listening and seeing my dog get bit by another was extremely frightening and it made me feel powerless.

P36: No

P37: One of my dog's got ran over, but survived.

P38: No

P39: She would pee around the house when she was a kitten.

P40: Yes! Buster-dog- tried to bite a little girl.

P41: We got a cat from the SPCA and it died of leukemia 3 months later.

P42: No

P43: No

P44: No

P45: No

P46: Yes, my cat got ran over and ended up dying when I moved away to college.

P47: No

P48: No

P49: Nope

P50: Not really, only one who was put down, and when they were sick.

P51: Yes- 1 cat, Maggie would turn mean all of a sudden and just scratch, Daisy's death was really hard and Floppy (bunny) was more hassle than he was worth.

P52: Yes, the cat, she seemed to always be angry and scratch us- the dog and cat hated each other also.

P53: Yes- T-Kitty didn't like me and I mistreated her as a child- I don't know which came first.

P54: Just losing one…

P55: Well, my cat ate my baby iguana which made me sad, but I would consider that a more negative experience for Julio my Iguana.

P56: Nope

P57: Only involving deaths

P58: No

P59: No, but I'm terrified of dogs- other people's dogs who bark and bite!

P60: No

P61: Got bit in the lip by my grandparent's dog and had stitches, but it didn't faze my love for dogs, just for that one.

P62: After the first one died, I stopped getting really upset. Slowly turn off emotions towards them.

P63: Yes… the 2 cats we had get hit by a car one not too long after the other.

P64: The cat my parents have now is a real bitch- she hisses at me every time I come home- she non-affectionate with me.

P65: No

P66: Not really

P67: I have had 5 die, that was not very pleasant.

P68: They eventually caused stress because they started urinating on things like couches and rugs and a horse riding accident. I was in the hospital for a week and afraid to ride after that.

P69: I was bit by a cat when I was 2.

P70: Lead to frustrating times- accidents

P71: No- Well, actually, Yes- I don't like cats and I had to sit for my roommate's cat- it was annoying.

P72: Yes, my parents gave away our pig because he stank and I was very attached to him. One of our dogs killed our squirrel (kind of by accident.)

P73: The death of my cats was very hard! My mother gave my dog away when I went to school and I've always hated her for that.

P74: My hamsters were not friendly and we never could play with or touch them. We gave them away.

P75: No

P76: No- just having to give them away is hard.

P77: No

P78: Yes, but not with my own, I have been bitten or attacked by other people's pets- cat, dogs, hamsters.

P79: My first dog bit me on my upper lip and caused me to get stitches. It was my fault though, so it didn't make us get rid of him.

P80: No

P81: No

P82: No

P83: Only giving away my dog.

P84: Pets dying.

P85: Just when one passed away. Also, just had to put my 14-year old dog to sleep this weekend.

P86: Only when they die.

P87: Except when they died.

P88: No

P89: No

P90: Nope, sure didn't.

P91: No

P92: Only when they died- added stress.

P93: Just scratches when I played too rough/teased the cats.

P94: No, other than one time when our box turtle bit and wouldn't let go of my 6-year old brother.

P95: Yes, they would scratch or bite

P96: When our dog Mel disappeared. Our parents told us she ran away but she was actually run over by a car.

P97: My cat died a few years ago- and one of my dogs died last year.

P98: I was bit by a dog once while running but I didn't know the dog or the house from which it came. The bite was not serious.

P99: Yes- Buttons- she bit the whole family- she was put down.

P100: Not my pets, but I have been bitten several times at the vet hospital I work at.

P101: Yes, we had a dog that ate the whole kitchen.

P102: Not one of my own!

9. Have you ever felt loved by a pet? If so, in what ways?

P1: N/A

P2: N/A

P3: Yes, when she bats at my legs and curls up next to me in bed at night.

P4: Yes, I had a bird last year and it was the sweetest birdie. It would nibble on my ear and tweet back at me.

P5: Definitely-even though I never had a pet I grew up with one, with my babysitter who always came near and sit next to me.

P6: N/A

P7: Yes.

P8: What does "love" mean? No.

P9: Not really.

P10: No.

P11: Yes, can't explain.

P12: Yes, they always come to you where you are.

P13: Yes, they always wanted to play.

P14: Yes, when I play with him, walk him, even bathe him. He licks our fingers affectionately very often.

P15: No, I don't think so.

P16: Yes, dogs coming to me, happy to see me, wanting to play, sleeping with me.

P17: Yes, they show affection when you walk into the room.

P18: I suppose, Amber and I would always be together during the day.

P19: Yes, it's hard to explain if you don't have a/or have never had a pet. You can just sense it. They are always so happy when you get home, etc.

P20: Yes, when I come home on college breaks.

P21: N/A

P22: Yes, when I rub my dog's belly.

P23: Yes, when I hurt my knee, the eldest cat always stayed near me.

P24: Yes, in uncomplicated animal ways.

P25: Yes.

P26: Yeah, my dog always craved my attention.

P27: Yes, if I got hurt my dog would sit next to me and lick my arm.

P28: Our current dog is a Cockapoo, half cocker/ half poodle, he is very affectionate and protective of the family.

P29: Absolutely, my pets have been very loving- they look for me when I am gone and spend time with me when I am sad. Pets act excited to see me.

P30: Yes, my cat nuzzles and massages my head with his paws.

P31: Yes- I know Rudy loves me because he sleeps with me at night and purrs when I come home.

P32: Yes, when my Bassett hound got ran over, my Pomeranian came and sat in my lap and just sat there with me.

P33: Yes, I feel my dog loves me because he runs to me when I get home and sleeps in my room.

P34: Yes, when a pet is scared and runs to me, sleeping with me, licking me.

P35: Yes, my dog loves me no matter what. In high school she was there when I felt alone.

P36: Yes, one dog that I had knew when something was wrong with me and would lay in my lap to comfort me.

P37: Yes, they are very caring by snuggling with you and I feel loved when they want attention or want to play with me.

P38: Yes, misses me when I am away, reacts to my emotions, etc.

P39: Yes, she would sleep with me at night and purr when I petted her, she even would lick my face.

P40: Yes! They show affection by sleeping with you or licking.

P41: My dog shows love to our family by sitting with us when we are watching TV.

P42: Yes, protected.

P43: I've felt loved by others' pets: my neighbor's dog, my best friend's cat, and my boyfriend's snake.

P44: Yes, when they haven't seen you for a little while and they are very happy to have you around.

P45: Yes, my dog would follow me around every time I was home. He would come and sleep in my room also.

P46: Yes, my dog and cat that we have now love on me.

P47: Yes, cause my cats always laid with me on the couch and comforted me when I cried.

P48: Yes, my cat would sit by the door and wait for me to come home and he only.

P49: Yes, always slept with me and always happy to see me, even when I went away to college.

P50: I feel loved by my dog. He's always happy to see me and really seems to know when I'm sad. He's extra nice when I am down, laying close, kissing, etc.

P51: Yes- when they cuddle up to you, you feel wanted. I love when Sable-my cat-purrs because it shows she's enjoying my company.

P52: Yes, when playing with them, when they lick you and get excited to see me.

P53: Yes- Rosi loves us, Eve loved us, but was too smart to get "mushy" they look at you and you know.

P54: Definitely- 2 of the cats we've had have been especially comforting, my cat now always stayed by my mom during her chemo-aftermath like he knew something was wrong.

P55: Yes, their attentiveness, and desire to cuddle, I'm not a very "touchy feely" person, but I like cuddling with my dogs.

P56: I always felt loved by Bingo, she always wanted to be with me. We ate together and I shared my food with her. She always slept with me.

P57: Yes, as their dependant.

P58: Yes, my dogs would always get really excited when I would come home from college.

P59: Yes, she is a great friend…even though we can't talk to each other…I can tell she appreciates me…I'm her caretaker…she was abandoned as a kitten…she is also a great listener.

P60: Yes, as mentioned before, always felt like I had someone to talk too, play with and cuddle with, especially with Nora.

P61: Oh yes, when they follow you around and get excited when they see you.

P62: My cat would come up to me and wants my attention.

P63: Yes…excited to see me, follows me around the house, cuddles with me in bed, and gives me dog kisses.

P64: Yes, Mark would come and sit by the bathtub every time I took a bath and would follow me around all the time.

P65: Yes, she was just always around and would sleep with you.

P66: I think all my pets loved me. I fed them ☺

P67: I have felt loved by my cat because when I was little and upset (crying) he would always come rub against me.

P68: Yes, just from all the affection they give and the support, they're always there.

P69: Yes, the way they come up to you and want you to pet them or when I've been sad and my dog would lick my face.

P70: Yeah, when she is excited to see me.

P71: Yes, dogs are loving and they go with our mood swings-they are just so patient and lovable.

P72: Yes, especially the dog I have now, that is just mine, she gets excited when I come home, she follows me around and she is very affectionate, licks, sits/lays with/on me.

P73: Of course, Babe, my dog, was my baby. I loved her to death and she depended on me. Purry was also quite dependent, he was afraid of crossing the yard and he'd meow until I walked with him across it.

P74: Yes- they rely on you. They are dependent on you, sort of like a child.

P75: They are always happy to see you and want to play.

P76: Yes, because they cuddle with you and want to be played with and follow you around wake you up when they know it's time.

P77: Can't feel loved by a frog and I did not have the dog long enough to remember.

P78: I feel very loved by my dog and all of my cats. My cats will brush up against me and kiss my nose when I come home from school.

P79: Plenty of times when I have had a bad day I swear they can sense that because my dog and cat have curled up and loved on me for hours.

P80: Yes, companion.

P81: Yes, my cat, Baby, always waits for me at the door and cries for me to love him as soon as I come home.

P82: Yes, you can tell that they enjoy your company.

P83: Yes, but my dogs and cat because they could recognize me. I also felt that way with my hamster.

P84: My dogs now- they get so excited to see me when I come home.

P85: Yes- when they sought me out, came to sit by me.

P86: Yes just by being around them.

P87: Yes, my dog Keiser loved me a lot, he always slept on my bed, ran to me when I came home and gave me kisses!

P88: Yes, my cat and dogs act like they love me by greeting me when I come home.

P89: Yes, our dog, I felt she loved us and was always excited to see my family and I.

P90: Yes, I loved when my dogs would welcome me when I came home and how my guinea pig squeals for me to pick him up.

P91: Yes, when my cat comes when I call.

P92: Yes, my cat shed. She crawls on my lap, rubs up against you to be petted.

P93: Yes, the little cat of mine knows when I come home from school, and yelps at me when I talk to her.

P94: Yes, my dog because she needs me to survive and looks to me as someone who takes care of her and as a friend because we travel together.

P95: Yes, they always act with love. Always happy when they see you, always wanting to be near you.

P96: I have felt loved by their need for me to take care of them and love them.

P97: Absolutely- dogs are so lovable- they truly adore you.

P98: Yes, the cat would come and wake me up in the morning and then sit on the end of my bed all day.

P99: Yes, Toby, when I go home for breaks, he still remembers me and is beside himself because he hasn't seen me in so long-shakes and whimpers.

P100: Of course, they snuggle with me when I'm upset or angry, they always run to the door all happy to see me, and they pout when I go on vacations.

P101: Yes, by the cats when they want something.

P102: Yes, when I'm laying sick on the bed, it's my puppy who comes to cuddle me! Quincy always knows when I need to be alone or not.

10. In what ways was the relationship you had with a pet similar or different from any relationships you had with family members?

P1: N/A

P2: N/A

P3: Yes, comforting relationship with pet. Difficult to compare that to family.

P4: I don't know.

P5: The pet that I knew will always be special because they will always remind me of my babysitters-who were a special part of my life.

P6: N/A

P7: I never loved my pet like a family member cause I was too young.

P8: Pets usually had problems communicating.

P9: Most of the times the pet was just perceived as more work.

P10: Called them by name, they kept me company.

P11: Dunno- I don't really think about it.

P12: Probably more affection with the pet actually.

P13: It was different.

P14: Similar, he can't talk though.

P15: I never argued with a pet.

P16: The pets never asked me to do anything I didn't want to do.

P17: You care for the pet well being but not at the same level.

P18: I don't think my relationship for pets were similar to any of my relationships with family.

P19: Didn't have to walk any family members.

P20: She's annoying at times and other times she's cool.

P21: N/A

P22: Not similar.

P23: They don't talk back.

P24: Not at all.

P25: N/A

P26: They (pet) could never criticize me.

P27: My dog couldn't talk to me and find out why I was upset.

P28: Our pet is very loving just like the family members are.

P29: I had and do have better relationships with my pets than I do with my family members.

P30: I always feel like I'm at home around my pets. I also feel like I'm at home where I belong with my family.

P31: N/A

P32: They were not as close as my relationships with my family.

P33: It was similar because I feel loved and he notices when I'm around.

P34: N/A

P35: My dog was nonjudgmental and she's funny so she could always make me laugh. She is always there to hug and love. This is similar to a sibling or parent I think.

P36: My family was there for me in every way but my dog is my comfort and family away from home.

P37: Not as close and personal, but similar.

P38: N/A

P39: It was different because we couldn't talk to one another.

P40: They are always there like any other family member-I miss my pets while at RU-just as much as I miss my parents.

P41: It is similar because like people dogs have needs. She also shares emotions like a real person.

P42: Played with, went on runs with.

P43: The similarities were mutual regard and respect, but the difference (and this made the relationship more special) was that the pets and I had no verbal communication and therefore no bickering, shouting, or misunderstanding.

P44: It was more consistent but was just as beneficial.

P45: Sometimes my dog was a little more comforting than my family members.

P46: They seem to know when you are down just like people.

P47: They were always around and I could play with them.

P48: N/A

P49: Similar because they live with you and know you and your emotions.

P50: It was similar than relationships with other people just unspoken, unyielding, and needed no real work to maintain.

P51: My dad can have trouble handling his anger-he just looses his temper (not in an abusive way), but he made me fearful of him, and Sable was often fearful of my dad, but in late years dad is Sable's favorite person and likewise, my relationship with dad is really good too.

P52: I never really got upset with my dog where as I did with my family.

P53: Not similar- pets not elevated to family member status- comparison would not be applicable.

P54: A pet can't talk back so you can spill you guts or confess anything without judgment or argument. I think my pets were comparable to a relationship with a sibling.

P55: Nurturing relationship similar to mother-daughter relationship with dog when mother was sick.

P56: My relationship with Bingo was similar to that with my family members due to communication. There was always open communication.

P57: Trust, love, co-dependency, responsible to each other.

P58: My pets wouldn't talk back to me or tell anything to other people.

P59: It's a difficult type of relationship, I fell responsible for my cats- a caretaker-of course, I guess I also tend to take on caretaking roles with my family members too- so in that respect it is similar.

P60: Similar to relationships with family members- especially my mom- loving, but superficial.

P61: I guess I could be seen as a dog and my father the owner. We love each other, we're loyal to each other, have fun, etc. But if he verbally abused me it was bad, but we'd get over it and return to normal.

P62: How I react to their death, I do separate myself from people that way too.

P63: Chance and I have such a close relationship that I guess it could resemble the relationship between me and my dad-trust, love, etc.

P64: My "relationship" with pets can not be compared to my relationship with my family.

P65: Same, because I could talk to her about things and I could talk to my parents-different in that I could tell her things I couldn't tell my parents because she wouldn't repeat what I said.

P66: N/A

P67: I show my cats minimal attention due to lack of time and effort which is similar to my father.

P68: Again just affectionate and supportive, like my parents. It was different though because with my parents I'm their child, I have to obey them, but not with my pets, they had no authority.

P69: Similar in that I would play with them and talk to them.

P70: She gets sad when we leave-happy when we come back-always there.

P71: My relation with my pet was unlike anything I had with my family.

P72: The dog never stays mad at me, even when I discipline her, she holds no grudges. I never feel any negativity from her at all-she never hurts my feelings.

P73: I could be the caregiver with them. I could spoil them. It was something I never had with anyone else.

P74: Although I love my pets, I love my family much more.

P75: N/A

P76: I never fight with my pets and like my family, they are always there to talk with about anything; granted pets can't talk back ☺

P77: N/A

P78: The relationship I had with my pets were never similar to those with my family members. I never isolated myself from my family to be with my pets.

P79: My parents took care of me by feeding me, taking me out to the park to play, and taking me to the doctor when I was sick. I do all that for my dog now.

P80: You can talk to them and they don't talk back.

P81: N/A

P82: Similar in that you care for each other, but different in the forms of communication.

P83: I love my pet (dog) like she is part of the family.

P84: I can tell my dogs things and not get judged.

P85: As strange as it may be, I could talk out loud to my pet-relieved stress, helped me talk out things in my own mind.

P86: I can talk to my pets about things going on in my life when I couldn't tell anyone else about relationships with boyfriends and major college choices.

P87: Keiser and I were always together. I liked him better then my family most of the time.

P88: The pet never talks back or gives you grief about your problems.

P89: I talked to our dog, but it wouldn't talk back, like the rest of my family would. But when I was sad she knew and comforted me.

P90: Pets were fun because you could talk to them without them butting in which was a help.

P91: You can always talk to animals cause they can't tell your secrets. Growing up, it's nice to be able to do that. I didn't tell my parents or sisters anything.

P92: I treat my pets like family members. Sleep where I sleep, has free roam of the house.

P93: They were in many ways the same- loving, generous, gracious at times, made you mad or sad, just like family members.

P94: Well obviously she or any pet I have don't talk back, so sometimes when you're upset they can sense that and provide comfort in their own way.

P95: Unconditional love.

P96: Sometimes you are able to ignore a pet where you can't do that with a person.

P97: Actually better sometimes- dogs don't stay made, and it's hard to stay made at a dog!

P98: We loved her like she was a member of the family.

P99: N/A- have had a practically perfect relationship with my family- can't really be related to the pets.

P100: My family loves me unconditionally as my pets do but, my animals are not nearly as quick to be frustrated with me as my family can sometimes be.

P101: N/A

P102: I almost believe the relationships with pets can be much more intense than with people. With people you have all these beliefs, feelings, and sometimes bad experiences, but with pets it's all about love all the time.

11. How have pets helped you feel better about yourself?

P1: N/A

P2: N/A

P3: Not really applicable, Kitty has made me a happier person in general though.

P4: They only make me feel good. They are friendly and lively.

P5: Simple- they remind me to be simple.

P6: N/A

P7: Not sure.

P8: By assuring me that I am more intelligent than them.

P9: No.

P10: Haven't.

P11: Gave me someone to focus on when I felt blue.

P12: Something to play with when others aren't around.

P13: No.

P14: I suppose.

P15: Probably not.

P16: They bring happiness in your life by being a friend to you and protecting you (dogs in particular.)

P17: Showed me that I can handle the responsibility.

P18: No.

P19: Learned to love and respect more than humans, responsibility.

P20: I'm allergic to them, so they generally make me feel sick.

P21: Just being able to take good care about the pet.

P22: Have not.

P23: Show affection.

P24: Companionship helped when sad.

P25: Responsible, getting lots of love from them.

P26: They always seem to love you and never judge you.

P27: My dog is always happy which makes me happy.

P28: Yes, our dog is always there and is happy all the time, he loves to play.

P29: They have been friends who will listen to me and my problems. They help build self-esteem and confidence from the relationships we share.

P30: I feel better about myself because whenever I walk into the room my cats run up and rub on legs.

P31: It gives me the chance to be a nurturer and I like knowing that something needs me.

P32: N/A

P33: I don't think they have except to show I can take care of things.

P34: No

P35: My dog loves me no matter what and that has made me feel good about myself.

P36: They just make you happy and help you enjoy life.

P37: Make me feel loved and wanted.

P38: Cared no matter what, always there for me.

P39: By loving me when I felt like everyone else was mad at me.

P40: You can talk and they don't yell back.

P41: My dog is very loving so her just coming to me when I'm upset makes me feel better!

P42: Liked them.

P43: Unconditional love was great for my self-esteem, and so was the responsibility.

P44: Yes.

P45: No.

P46: N/A

P47: They make me have brighter days, cheer me up.

P48: Loved.

P49: Never able to say anything negative about me, always there for me.

P50: Always like me, try to make me feel better when I'm sad.

P51: Sometimes when I'm upset I go talk to Abby and Sable and curl up to them- may sound dumb- but it helps.

P52: They make me forget about problems- I can just have fun with my friends.

P53: They make me feel responsible and active.

P54: Just by comforting me and other members- they can make you feel loved.

P55: I'm glad I'm not so furry- ha- their always kind.

P56: Bingo really boosted my self esteem. She kept me happy at all times.

P57: Can't explain it, they just do.

P58: Through their unconditional love.

P59: Someone who listens to you and doesn't talk back....but you feel like they understand.

P60: Gave me a sense of self worth and importance and was there for me when I was feeling down.

P61: Because you always have something that will love you unconditionally.

P62: Sometimes an ear to listen when I need it. Soothing.

P63: Always there for me when I need him and he always lends a listening ear even if he doesn't understand what I'm saying.

P64: Never thought about it.

P65: Make me feel loved.

P66: N/A

P67: I enjoy feeling needed.

P68: By knowing that I'm important to someone (something no matter what I do)

P69: Yes, you have someone to take care of, you feel needed and loved.

P70: Security, comfort.

P71: When I used to talk to my dog it made me feel like I was someone important to him- he would follow me around and wait for me after school.

P72: It's nice to have someone (or thing) who depends on you and loves you more than anyone else.

P73: I was needed.

P74: I guess by being able to take care of them, knowing they need you.

P75: I believe pets give you a sense of responsibility and often, in the case of a dog, they can make people very happy, loved, and give good company.

P76: When I am sad or feeling alone I have someone there and it makes me feel better.

P77: N/A

P78: They have made me realize my patience and soft-natured personality. Most animals respond really well to me.

P79: Made me feel very wanted and needed.

P80: N/A

P81: Knowing my cat will always love me makes me feel good.

P82: Comforting when you are sad, do something funny to make you laugh.

P83: They recognize me.

P84: They always make me smile because they always act happy to see me.

P85: All of them.

P86: They love me when I am having a bad day.

P87: Keiser made me happy knowing he was excited to see me.

P88: They have made me feel loved and given me responsibility.

P89: N/A

P90: Pets have made me feel better about myself because they have made me feel loved and welcome all of the time.

P91: Since coming to college I have learned I can keep a fish alive for 8 months and counting, I guess that makes me responsible.

P92: Nice to cuddle with when you are feeling down, or sad.

P93: They calm me and ease me from a stressful day, and are always there to listen even though they can't talk back.

P94: They provide an undying friendship with no strings attached-just love!!

P95: They constantly want attention from you.

P96: The constant love they need so you feel wanted.

P97: Physically, do things outside with them; also loveable and are just GREAT!!

P98: Sometimes.

P99: They (the dogs) are just always happy to see you.

P100: Both by loving me unconditionally and needing me.

P101: They show love by giving you their attention.

P102: They remind me that I can brighten someone's day by just smiling.

12. Were the pets in your house considered family members, if so, how?

P1: N/A

P2: N/A

P3: Yes, took pictures of animals, set play time, lots of toys, etc.

P4: No

P5: No pets.

P6: N/A

P7: Yes.

P8: Yes.

P9: No.

P10: Yes, now that I have left for school, my cats have taken over the house.

P11: Pretty much in many ways, the fact they couldn't feed themselves and couldn't be trusted to walk themselves hindered that.

P12: Sometimes, I remember when one was in a family picture.

P13: No.

P14: Yes, (read above)- Very well, treated as almost a member of the family. Scruffy has frequented a certain chair (a lazy boy) so often that it has become "his chair."- Bring comfort, friendliness, and love to our family.

P15: No, they weren't considered equal to family members, but they were close.

P16: Yes.

P17: Yes, they had Christmas gifts, birthdays and are part of family life.

P18: I can't explain how, but they were.

P19: Yes, because they are!

P20: Umm...kinda, she gets a stocking for Christmas.

P21: Yes.

P22: No.

P23: Perhaps, took care of them and played with them.

P24: No.

P25: Yes- they were even in some family pictures.

P26: Yes, they were always involved in things like Birthdays and Christmas.

P27: Yes, she has been in every family photo and every Christmas card.

P28: Close, pretty much, we talk to our dog like he is a person.

P29: Yes, they were like people and have the same temperaments. Ex: my cat eats when we do.

P30: Yes, our pets are considered family. They get people food, presents, and their own stockings at Christmas.

P31: Yes- they were well taken care of and loved.

P32: Not really.

P33: They were by me because I took care of them.

P34: Yes, (see question 4)- Pets were treated as family members-slept in our beds, on sofa watching TV, went on trips.

P35: Yes- my father was the only man!- then my mom, me, my sister and dog (female). My dog has her own Christmas stocking- that is a symbol you're part of my family.

P36: Yes. They were always allowed inside and have their own beds. We have even had a family picture taken with them.

P37: Yes, they had names and we took them places.

P38: Yes, mom always needs them near her, we have to make sure they are happy and taken care of.

P39: Yes, she was treated very well.

P40: Yes! They were treated just like any other.

P41: We consider our dog a member of the family, she is included in all activities especially summer trips.

P42: Yes, always said I had 1 brother, 1 sister, and dog.

P43: No.

P44: Yes, they were treated just as we were, but they didn't eat our food.

P45: Yes, he basically did everything that we did.

P46: Yes, they just were.

P47: Yes, they were allowed to lay on top of the dinner table when we ate, could go anywhere in the house, we took them on car trips, if were sick took care of them.
P48: Yes, they were treated just like kids, taken to the vet, bought stuff for him.
P49: Yes, because they went on vacation with me.
P50: Yes, sleep on beds, get lots of treats and love, hard to get mad at them.
P51: Pretty much-especially Daisy- we had a really hard time loosing him.
P52: Answered above- they make me forget about problems- I can just have fun with my friends.
P53: So-So is the longest running pet. She counts.
P54: Of course- they have stockings at Christmas and are in our family pictures.
P55: Yes, respected, protected.
P56: Yes, Bingo was an indoor pet. She would go with us to my grandparents' houses. She ate people food. Slept in my bed.
P57: Yes- they got Christmas presents and everything.
P58: Yes, through the way that they were treated so well.
P59: Sort of….but my dad will always see them as cats…my mom and I are closer to them.
P60: Yes- were kind and compassionate and loving.
P61: No, not really, but my dog now is for me.
P62: Yes, they were important, they got love and attention too.
P63: Yes…write cards to each other from out pets, given table scraps, loved, and treated well.
P64: Yes- (see question 4)…..They were treated like one of the family (a child to my parents and a brother/sister to me and my sister)
P65: Yes, ate table food, sleep with my parents.
P66: No.
P67: Not really.
P68: Yes, like they were my kids.
P69: Yes, they would get presents at Christmas time, special treats.
P70: Yes- treated well- ate better than we did!!
P71: Yes; they were included in all of family events such as vacations, meals, every trip.
P72: Not really- they were loved but not spoiled.
P73: Sure, Christmas gifts.
P74: Yes, my dad refers to Molly as my "sister."
P75: N/A
P76: Yes, just because we are so close with them. We feed them and take care of them.
P77: No.
P78: The pets were considered family members by my brothers and mom and I, not by my dad.
P79: Yes. They got fed as well as we did.
P80: Yes, like a sister.
P81: Yes.
P82: No.
P83: Yes, we even had stockings for our dog.

P84: Yes- they get presents on all holidays (birthdays too) and they are called the babies.
P85: Yes- to a great extent. Well fed, well housed, well loved.
P86: Yes, they actually come in and out of the house like a regular family member.
P87: Yes, Keiser and the cats had their own beds, toys, and Christmas stockings.
P88: Yes, they ate the same food we did and were allowed in the house to sleep or do whatever.
P89: Yes.
P90: Yes, they were all considered to be family members and were always included.
P91: No not at all, my mom insisted they stay outside, but we still took good care of them.
P92: Yes- always. They are treated extremely well.
P93: Yes, they were either like my children, or my brothers/sisters.
P94: Yes, they were babies or brothers and sisters.
P95: Yes, they were treated with much love, had our last name, received presents.
P96: Yes, the dog comes on vacation with us. Gets Christmas presents.
P97: Yes- in many ways. Ex. We sign our greeting cards with our <u>and</u> their names.
P98: Yes, we cared for her like she was one of us.
P99: Yes, Toby thinks he's a person; the puppy, Havoc, at my apartment, gets to sleep in the beds and is always being pampered.
P100: Yes they are, they receive the same amount of love, care, and attention as my family members, as well as serving their own role within my family's structure.
P101: Yes, we talked to them like people.
P102: Yes ☺ They go on vacation with us, eat the same food, and sleep in our beds.

CPSIA information can be obtained
at www.ICGtesting.com
Printed in the USA
LVHW091002091121
702847LV00004B/33